The GOLDEN BOOK ENCYCLOPEDIA

NEW REVISED EDITION

VOLUME 6—EROSION TO GEYSER

IN SIXTEEN ACCURATE, FACT-FILLED VOLUMES

DRAMATICALLY ILLUSTRATED WITH MORE

THAN 6,000 COLOR PICTURES

ESPECIALLY DESIGNED FOR
YOUNG GRADE-SCHOOL CHILDREN
ACCURATE AND AUTHORITATIVE
ENTERTAININGLY WRITTEN AND ILLUSTRATED
TO MAKE LEARNING AN ADVENTURE

BY BERTHA MORRIS PARKER

FORMERLY OF THE LABORATORY SCHOOLS, UNIVERSITY OF CHICAGO
RESEARCH ASSOCIATE, FIELD MUSEUM OF NATURAL HISTORY

GOLDEN PRESS • NEW YORK

REVISED EDITION, 1969
Library of Congress Catalog Card Number: 69-16035

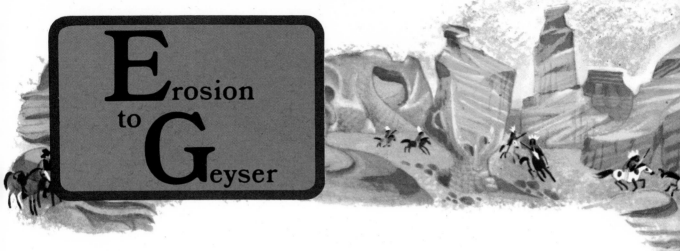

EROSION Ever since the earth's beginnings, a battle has been going on between the land and the sea. In some places the land is winning. New land is being made, or old land is being pushed higher. In other places the sea is winning. The land is being worn away and carried to the sea.

The wearing away of land is called erosion. Wind, waves, ice, and running water do most of the wearing away.

Wind carrying grains of sand can wear away even solid rock. Windblown sand sometimes carves rock into strange shapes.

Waves can wear away solid rock, too, if they have weapons. The weapons waves use are sand and pebbles.

Rivers of ice gouge deep valleys. They act like great plows and push rocks and soil ahead of them.

But in the battle between land and sea the chief fighter on the side of the sea is running water. Rainwater, on its way to the sea, does more wearing away of land than wind and waves and ice together.

For hundreds of millions of years erosion has gone on. Whole ranges of mountains have been worn down. Deep valleys like the Grand Canyon have been cut.

Loose soil can be worn away much faster than solid rock. The great Mississippi River dumps two million tons of soil into the Gulf of Mexico every day. No wonder farmers now think of erosion as the greatest enemy of their soil.

Erosion goes on faster if the soil is bare than if it is covered with grass or trees. Roots help hold soil in place. Erosion goes on faster on hillsides than on level ground if the soil is all the same and is being farmed in the same way. Knowing these things helps farmers fight erosion.

Soil likely to be blown away by the wind is better used for pastureland than for cultivated fields. Trees can be raised on steep slopes. There are different ways of protecting hillside land used for field crops: Grass can be planted between strips of

Streams carve the land into gullies and valleys.

crops such as corn and potatoes. Fields on hillsides can be plowed horizontally—across the slope instead of up and down it. Hillsides can be terraced.

A gully in a field is always a danger sign. If the farmer does nothing about it, the gully is sure to grow larger. A gully has been known to swallow up a whole farm.

Erosion has already ruined millions of acres of farmland. Some of this damage cannot be undone. But we can build up some of the eroded land again, and we can do a great deal to save the good land we have left. (See CONSERVATION; GRAND CANYON; MISSISSIPPI RIVER; SOIL.)

ESKIMOS The northern shores of North America touch the cold Arctic Ocean. The land along them is barren. The winters are long and very cold. The region might be called Eskimo land, for most of the people there are Eskimos. Eskimo land includes the ice-capped island of Greenland and a part of the Siberian coast as well.

Living where no crops can be raised and where winter temperatures are far below zero is not easy. But the Eskimos are clever. They long ago worked out ways of living that were fitted to their cold, barren land. The Eskimo earned the name "the man who can make the most out of nothing."

Eskimos learned to make snug houses out of snow. A snowhouse is called an igloo. A long tunnel leads into a snowhouse. A skylight of clear ice lets in light. It is warm inside a snowhouse. It may even be uncomfortably hot. An oil lamp lights up the house and also warms it. The floor is higher than the floor of the entrance. The higher floor keeps cold air from pouring in the door and driving warm air out.

An Eskimo may build many snowhouses during one winter. For some Eskimos are nomads. They wander from place to place.

In some places Eskimos learned to build winter homes of driftwood and bank up dirt around them. In the summer they could set up tents of skin to live in.

The name Eskimo means "eater of raw meat." The Eskimos do eat much of their meat uncooked. This fact may help explain why they have been able to get along without fresh fruits and vegetables.

Much of the meat Eskimos eat comes from the sea. Fish and seals and whales furnish most of it. Long ago the Eskimos learned how to make harpoons and spears to help them get food from the sea.

The seal has been especially important to the Eskimo. Every part of the animal was put to use except the bones and the bladder. The Eskimo thought that the spirit of the seal would haunt him if he did not put the bones and the bladder back into the sea. The fat in the seal's body was good fuel. Seal meat made good food for both the Eskimo and his dogs. An Eskimo takes very good care of his dogs. They pull his sleds and help him hunt. Sealskin made warm, dry boots. It made a good covering

for the Eskimo's boats. It made harness for his dog team and leather strings for harpoons and—before the rifle replaced the bow and arrow—for bows.

Whales are much harder to catch than seals. Sometimes a whole village would go on a whale hunt. A captured whale was a real prize. The fat, or blubber, was the Eskimo child's candy. Whale fat is good body fuel and helped the Eskimos stand the cold. Whale meat is good to eat, and whalebone could be put to use in many ways.

The walrus has long been hunted, too, not so much for its meat as for its skin, its oil, and its tusks. The ivory made good heads for spears and harpoons.

The Eskimos could kill foxes and other land mammals for fur for warm clothing. He could hunt the caribou for its meat and its skin. Some Eskimos began raising reindeer. Reindeer furnish milk. They can also help with the work of pulling sledges.

Eskimos usually made their sledges from driftwood and whalebone. They learned to coat the runners with ice for traveling over stretches of rough ground. For going to sea they invented two different kinds of skin boats. One is a one-man boat called a kayak. An Eskimo fits snugly into his kayak. He can drive it with a paddle. A rough sea may turn a kayak upside down, but the man does not fall out. An Eskimo can use his paddle so skillfully that he is soon right side up again. The other skin boat of the Eskimos is called an umiak. It is much like a big rowboat.

Most Eskimos are cheerful and friendly. After a good hunt they sing, dance, and tell stories. The children are usually smiling even though they have few playthings. They are much petted by the grown-ups.

The Eskimos have lived in the Arctic for over 2,000 years. So far as anyone knows, they have never tried to leave their unfriendly land and find easier living farther south. Getting a living has been very hard, however. The Eskimos have not been increasing in number. Some college football stadiums are big enough to hold all the Eskimos there are in the world today with room to spare.

Some of the Eskimos still live much as their ancestors did. But others have learned many modern ways. Steel knives and spearheads have taken the place of bone and ivory weapons. There are well-stocked trading posts where Eskimos can buy or trade furs for such things as tea, guns, needles, tents, telescopes, and bubble gum. Many Eskimo boys and girls go to up-to-date schools and learn to speak English. Now that the Arctic is proving to be a storehouse of minerals, many Eskimos have well-paying and responsible jobs. Radios, record players, motorboats, and good frame houses are common over much of Eskimo land. If you were to go near an Eskimo home you might hear a familiar hit song coming from it. (See ALASKA; ARCTIC REGIONS; CANADA; GREENLAND.)

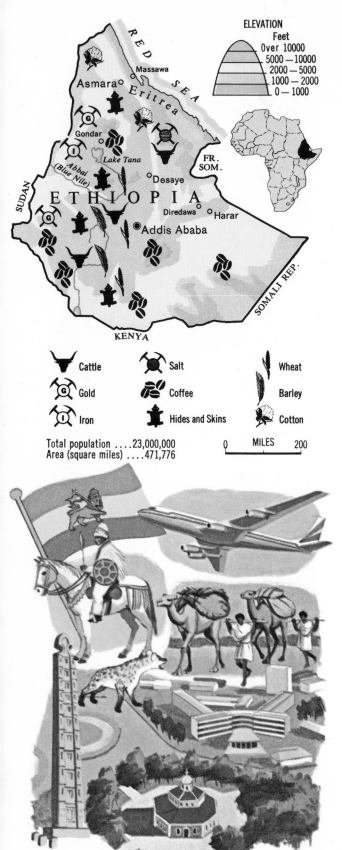

ELEVATION
Feet
Over 10000
5000 – 10000
2000 – 5000
1000 – 2000
0 – 1000

RED SEA
Massawa
Asmara
Eritrea
Gondar
Lake Tana
Abbai (Blue Nile)
SUDAN
ETHIOPIA
Dessye
FR. SOM.
Diredawa
Harar
Addis Ababa
SOMALI REP.
KENYA

Cattle
Gold
Iron
Salt
Coffee
Hides and Skins
Wheat
Barley
Cotton

Total population 23,000,000
Area (square miles) 471,776

MILES
0   200

ETHIOPIA As the small map shows, Ethiopia is in the eastern part of the big continent of Africa. It is an independent country ruled by an emperor.

Ethiopia was shut off from the rest of the world for so long that it was a land of mystery. Much of its border is very steep. Most of the country is a land of high plateaus and mountains. The surrounding land is mostly desert. Few roads or even caravan trails led into it. It did not touch the sea, and its rivers flow too fast to be good highways. Now it is no longer shut off and mysterious. Eritrea, on the shore of the Red Sea, has become a part of Ethiopia. And several airlines reach it.

Although the country is near the equator, some of its highest land is too cold for crops. Its lowlands are hot and dry. Most people of the lowlands are herders. They move their cattle, sheep, and goats from place to place to find good pasture. But farmers raise many kinds of crops on the plateau. They have fields of wheat, barley, corn, and teff, or love grass, the chief bread grain of the country. On some of the lower mountain slopes it is warm and rainy. Forests grow there. In them, coffee grows wild. Coffee is raised, too, on cleared slopes in the highlands. The country has chiefly coffee and hides to sell.

Ethiopia was long called backward. But it has been making much progress. Farmers still use cattle for plowing. Many goods are carried on mules or in oxcarts. But there are now two railroads and a number of good motor roads in the country. It has over 1,500 schools. There are 25,000 telephones, mostly in Addis Ababa, the capital, and 325,000 radios. Television was introduced in 1964. Addis Ababa has four newspapers, two in English and two in Amharic, the native language of many Ethiopians. And in 1967 Ethiopian Air Lines started the first African-operated, all-cargo service to Europe. Ethiopia's emperor, Haile Selassie I, has played an important part in African and world affairs. (See AFRICA.)

ETIQUETTE The word "etiquette" comes from a French word which first meant "little ticket." In France little tickets used to be given to the people who were going to take part in a public ceremony. On each person's ticket there were directions telling him just what to do during the ceremony. Thus etiquette came to mean the right way to act when you are with other people.

Every group of people has its rules of etiquette. Even savages do. But good manners in one group of people may not be good manners at all in another group.

An Eskimo guest smacks his lips after a meal to show that he has enjoyed it. We think that smacking the lips is impolite.

In Africa some tribesmen greet one another by saying, "How do you sweat?" To many such a question would be rude.

Shaking hands with a friend you meet is common in many parts of the world. But in some other regions people hold their own hands together instead. In many countries a man to be polite often takes off his hat. A native of Ghana, in Africa, however, lets his robe slip down off one shoulder.

When a visitor leaves us after a visit, we say, "Good-bye." "Good-bye" is short for "God be with you." When a visitor leaves a group of natives in New Guinea, the hosts wail and smear themselves with mud.

The people of the Far East eat in silence. To them it is bad manners to talk during a meal. We think that helping to carry on a conversation is an important part of good table manners.

The members of one tribe of Africa have what seems to other people a strange custom. They spit to show approval. A warrior of this tribe spits on a boy he sees for the first time. He spits in his hand before he picks up and uses a new weapon.

In Tibet it is etiquette to stick out one's tongue at the end of a visit. Doing so means to Tibetans that they have enjoyed the chance to talk together.

Thus manners differ throughout the world. But everywhere the rules of etiquette

Prehistoric Europeans

Hindu

Eskimos

American

Tibetans

WAYS OF GREETING

Ukrainian Girl

Colonial American

Medieval Knight

Japanese

Uganda

answer the same questions. Some of these questions are:

How should strangers be introduced?

How should friends greet each other?

How should older people be treated?

What are good table manners?

How should a person dress for different special occasions?

How do you show respect to rulers?

The most complicated rules of etiquette have to do with rulers. A story of King Louis XIII of France tells something about court etiquette in his time. The King once went to visit Cardinal Richelieu, who was ill. It was against the rules of etiquette for a cardinal to lie down while his king was either standing or sitting. There was only one thing to do—the King must lie down, too. He did, and the visit went smoothly.

There are, of course, no American kings and noblemen. But there is a president and there are governors and senators. Rules of etiquette tell how to act in the presence of these officials.

Why do we have to have rules of etiquette? Good manners help us get on smoothly with others. But why can't each person follow his own ideas of politeness?

The danger is that a person trying to be polite might be misunderstood. Suppose a traveler approaches the chieftain of a strange tribe. The chieftain waves his hand to greet him. The traveler may not understand the hand waving. He may think that the chieftain is summoning his warriors. Having rules of etiquette is a help because everyone understands them.

No one knows how all our rules of etiquette came to be. We know, however, how some came about, and we can make good guesses about others.

One rule of table manners says that a spoon should never be left standing in a cup. It is easy to see what is back of this rule. It would be easy to catch the spoon in a sleeve and upset the cup.

Another rule of etiquette says that no one should interrupt anyone who is talking.

This rule, too, is easy to understand. But most rules are not so easy to explain.

Here are some of the ideas people have of how some rules of etiquette came about.

The custom of shaking hands, some people think, began with prehistoric man. At first every man was the enemy of all others. A man carried a club to protect himself not only against wild animals but also against his fellowmen. In time men learned that they could be friends with one another. Each one now needed a clear way of showing others that he was friendly. What better way could there be than to drop his club and hold out his bare hand?

In the Middle Ages the faces of men in armor were hidden by the visors of their helmets. If a person in armor wished to show a person he met that he was a friend, he raised his visor or, better still, took off his helmet. Today men take off their hats.

The greeting, "How do you sweat?" is used in regions where fever is common. If a person is sick with a fever, his skin is likely to be dry. A moist skin is a good sign that a person is not ill. "How do you sweat?" is really like saying, "How are you?"

Some tribes believe that saliva is a protection against evil spirits. This idea explains why an African warrior may spit as a sign of approval.

It is bad manners to mop up your plate with a piece of bread or to pick up a piece of chicken with both hands. Doing so suggests that you are very hungry. These practices came to be bad manners because people did not want anyone to think that they had not been having enough to eat.

No matter how our rules of etiquette came to be, people are likely to make fun of us if we break them. If we broke very many, probably no one would have much to do with us. For this reason many people are more careful about following the rules of good manners than about following some laws. Many people would rather be caught running a red light than reading a letter over somebody's shoulder.

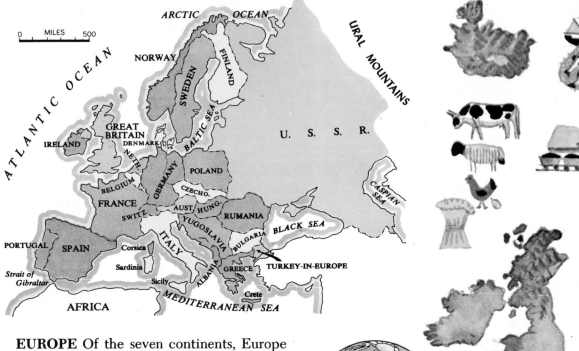

EUROPE Of the seven continents, Europe is the next to the smallest. Only Australia is smaller. Europe is very little larger than the United States.

Sometimes Europe is called a part of the great continent of Eurasia and not a separate continent at all. As anyone would guess from the name, Eurasia includes Asia, too. A map of the world shows that Europe is really a peninsula that stretches westward from Asia.

Maps show, too, that Europe has several peninsulas of its own. Often it is called a peninsula of peninsulas. Norway and Sweden are in one of Europe's peninsulas. Denmark, Italy, Portugal, Spain, and Greece are other countries in other European peninsulas.

Though Europe is small as continents go, it is sometimes spoken of as the greatest continent. It has hundreds of millions of people. Only Asia has more. And Europeans have spread their ideas and ways of doing things far and wide in the world.

Europe is farther north than most people think. Its northern coast borders the Arctic Ocean. The capitals of Norway, Sweden, and Finland are farther north than Juneau, Alaska. The capitals of more

Calder Hall Atomic Power Plant in England

Hydroelectric Power Plant in Sweden

Lumbering in Norway

Threshing Grain by Old-fashioned
Methods in Greece

than 20 other countries in Europe are all farther north than Portland, Me. Among them are the famous big cities of London, Paris, and Brussels.

The climate of much of Europe is milder than anyone would expect for a land so far north. The part of the Atlantic Ocean near much of Europe is warmed by an ocean current from far to the south. Winds that blow in from over the Atlantic are a big help. If it were not for those warm winds, most of the northern half of the continent would be good for little except hunting and herding. As it is, there are fine farms farther north than Labrador. And even along Europe's Arctic coast there are some ice-free ports.

Europe has anything but a smooth coastline. If the coast of Norway alone were pulled out into a straight line, it would reach from the Arctic to the equator. There are good harbors along Europe's very long coast. Many kinds of fish live not far from that coast. For centuries many people of Europe have taken to the sea. Good harbors and good fishing are reasons why.

This small continent has several mountain ranges. Of them all, the Alps, which center in Switzerland, are the most famous. Fortunately, no long, high range runs north from the Alps. Such a range would keep much of central Europe from getting the warm, moist winds from the Atlantic.

Many large rivers rise in Europe's mountains and flow to the sea. Among the most famous ones are the north-flowing Rhine, the east-flowing Danube and Po, and the south-flowing Rhone. Many of the rivers are good highways. In their valleys there

is much very fertile soil. Some of the rivers
have built deltas. Much of the Netherlands
(Holland) is on the big delta of the Rhine.
"The Rhine," people sometimes say, "built
the Netherlands."

In many places falls in the rivers are
used in making electricity to run machines
in factories. And Europe is rich in two
minerals needed in many factories and
mills—coal and iron. Those minerals are
found in Europe in a number of places
where it is not hard to mine them.

Since there are many countries in small
Europe, it goes without saying that at least
some of them are small. Italy, one of the
larger ones, is about the size of Arizona.
Belgium is only slightly larger than Mary-
land. The smallest country in Europe is
the smallest country in the world. It is the
State of Vatican City. But the eastern part
of Europe (about half the continent) is a
part of the biggest country in the world.
This is the Soviet Union. Most of this huge
country is in Asia. The State of Vatican City
is too small to show on many maps of Europe. So are six other countries. They are
Luxembourg, Andorra, Malta, Liechtenstein,
San Marino, and Monaco.

The people of Europe earn a living in
many different ways. In some countries

Fields of Flowers in the Netherlands

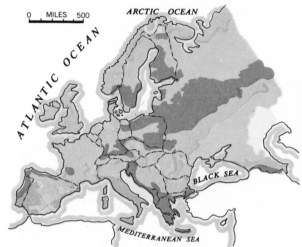

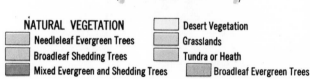

NATURAL VEGETATION
- Needleleaf Evergreen Trees
- Broadleaf Shedding Trees
- Mixed Evergreen and Shedding Trees
- Desert Vegetation
- Grasslands
- Tundra or Heath
- Broadleaf Evergreen Trees

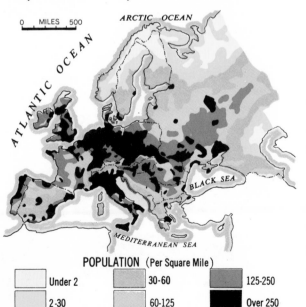

POPULATION (Per Square Mile)
- Under 2
- 2-30
- 30-60
- 60-125
- 125-250
- Over 250

Harvesting Grapes in Vineyards of France

CLIMATES

- Cool and Dry
- Subtropical, Dry
- Subtropical, Wet
- Temperate with Cool Summer
- Temperate with Warm Summer
- Subarctic
- Cold and Dry
- Hot and Dry
- Highlands

Skiing in the Swiss Alps

more than 25 of over 1,000,000 and four—London, Paris, Moscow, and Leningrad—of over 3,000,000.

Europeans have some problems that come from the fact that Europe is divided into more than 30 countries. The languages vary. Many Europeans have to know several. Laws and customs also differ. A number of the countries are crowded. They need more room for all their people.

Much of Europe's very long history is a story of struggle. Some of the struggles were between neighboring nations. Some peoples fought to acquire more land. Other

farming is the chief work. Other countries are chiefly industrial. Along the coasts fishing is important. In the mountains many work at lumbering. Europe's farms and fisheries do not produce as much food as its people need. Some must be brought from other lands. And European products must be sold to pay for this food and other products Europe wants from abroad. It takes millions of people to carry on Europe's trade. Since trade and manufacturing go on mostly in cities, it is no wonder that Europe has many big ones. There are

Busy Fishing Port of Italy

groups fought to hold on to what they had. There also were struggles with newcomers. Time after time through the centuries, peoples from dry central Asia pushed into Europe in search of rainier land. There have been a great many changes in the boundaries between different countries.

Scientists believe that people lived in Europe hundreds of thousands of years ago. Some of the very oldest fossils of *Homo sapiens* ("thinking man") that have been found were found in Europe. But happenings there in prehistoric times can only be guessed from such things as the tools and weapons found there since history began.

The first great civilizations in Europe were in Greece and Rome. In ancient times Greeks and Romans had many important ideas about art, literature, law, and religion. Those ideas spread to the west and

north over Europe. Many of them were among the ideas Europeans had when, many years later, America was discovered.

The first European people to settle in the New World were the Spanish. The second were the Portuguese, who settled in what is now Brazil. Most of the Spanish settlements were in South America, Mexico, and Central America. Today most people who live south of the United States in the Americas speak Spanish. About 40 years after the first Spanish settlement in what is now the United States, the English began making settlements there. People from other European countries made settlements in North America, too. But the English later controlled most of these settlements. English customs and language have spread not only through most of North America but through Australia and New Zealand, too. Today people from Europe live also in parts of Asia and Africa. Wherever they have gone they have spread European ideas, customs, and inventions.

Each year thousands of Americans visit Europe. They see reminders of Europe's long past and of the great works of its people. They feel much at home. They are in the wonderful part of the world from which the ancestors of most of them came. What they see and learn there helps them have a better understanding of their own country's story. (See CONTINENTS; ICE AGE.)

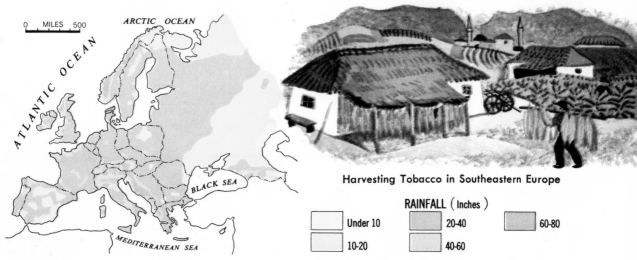

Harvesting Tobacco in Southeastern Europe

RAINFALL (Inches)

Under 10	20-40	60-80
10-20	40-60	

EVOLUTION When the earth was very young, scientists think, there were no living things on it at all. Then, perhaps a billion or more years ago, some living things appeared. They were very small—only one cell in size. They were simple, but they were also very important, for they were the ancestors of all the living things on earth today.

It took millions of millions of changes for the whale to come from the first living things. It took millions of millions of changes for the oak tree to be produced. It is hard to imagine how many changes it took to produce all of today's plants and animals. Scientists have a name for these countless changes. It is evolution.

The chief reason scientists believe in evolution is that they have studied fossils. Fossils are usually found in rocks. They are traces of the plants and animals of long ago. From fossils, scientists can tell that there was a time when all the plants and animals were very simple. Then, as ages passed, more-and-more-complicated plants and animals appeared. There are no fossils of birds and mammals and flowering plants except in rocks that are rather young, as rock ages go.

Fossils tell parts of the story of evolution very clearly. Fossils show that about 50 million years ago horses were no bigger than foxes and had four little hoofs on their front feet and three on the back feet. Their teeth were suited for eating only tender leaves. But, as millions of years went by, they changed little by little until they became the horses that we know.

By no means every part of the story of evolution is as clear as the story of the horse. But enough is clear to make scientists sure that all plants and animals came from the very first living things on the earth. (See EARTH HISTORY; FOSSILS; HORSES; LIFE THROUGH THE AGES.)

EXPERIMENTS Galileo, the famous Italian scientist, is often called the father of modern science. He has been given this name because he showed scientists a new way of finding things out. He showed them the method of experimenting.

Experimenting means simply testing or trying things out. Today it seems a perfectly natural thing to do. Boys and girls carry on many experiments in their science classes. But in Galileo's time most scholars thought that ancient writers had said all that there was to say about the different sciences. The scholars did not test the old ideas. They

Dawn Horse
24 in.

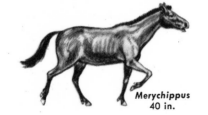

Mesohippus
24 in.

Merychippus
40 in.

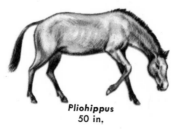

Pliohippus
50 in.

Equus—Modern Horse
60 in.

Iodine is being used as a test for starch. It produces a purple color if starch is present.

A simple electromagnet can be made with an iron nail and insulated wire. This homemade magnet is attracting paper clips.

did not try to find out anything new by experimenting.

Galileo showed that some of the old ideas were wrong and that much could be learned through experiments. Today experiments are an important part of a great many sciences. And some experiments can be called milestones. Galileo's experiments with falling bodies, Pasteur's with disease germs, and Mendel's with heredity are a few.

Experimenting must be done very carefully if it is to be worthwhile. And no one should depend too much on just one experiment. A scientist repeats an important experiment time after time and keeps careful records of his results.

No experiments today are carried on more carefully than those with new drugs. Before a new drug is sold, it is tried out for months or even years.

Experiments in the field of surgery are among the most important now being carried on. Other important experiments have to do with turning ocean water into fresh water, with getting new foods from the sea for the world's fast-growing population, and with fighting air and water pollution. Still others are concerned with everyday uses of atomic power and with space travel. (See GALILEO; MENDEL; PASTEUR.)

EXPLORERS The earth isn't really any larger now than it was thousands of years ago. But the part that people know about has grown bigger. Fifteen years ago the upper air and the floor of the deep sea were the only big parts of the earth that no one had ever visited. Now explorers have gone even there.

Explorers have set out on their travels for many different reasons. Some hoped to find great riches. Some wanted to discover new routes to such places as the Indies. Others went for adventure or to meet the challenge of "something there." Some explorers were missionaries. Some wanted to help build empires. And many have been eager to make new scientific discoveries.

Exploring unknown regions is never easy. Explorers suffer great hardships. Many have died before they could get back to tell what they had found.

It is not always easy to be sure of what past explorers actually found out. Many mixed stories they made up with true stories. But some of the strangest stories the early explorers told were true.

The following chart tells a little about some of the most famous explorers.

EXPLORER Nationality and Dates	EXPLORATION
LEIF ERICSON Norse	Leif the Lucky reached North America about 1000, nearly 500 years before the time of Columbus.
MARCO POLO Italian 1254—1324	Marco Polo traveled all over Asia. His book about his travels made other people want to go exploring.
HENRY the NAVIGATOR Portuguese 1394—1460	Henry the Navigator was a Portuguese prince. He improved ships and compasses and sent out explorers.
CHRISTOPHER COLUMBUS Italian 1451—1506	Columbus sailed across the Atlantic and reached the New World first in 1492. He made three later voyages.
AMERICUS VESPUCIUS Italian 1451—1512	Americus Vespucius sailed thousands of miles along the shores of the New World. The New World was named for him.
JOHN CABOT Italian 1450—1498	John Cabot was an Italian explorer who sailed in the service of England. He reached the shores of North America in 1497.
VASCO da GAMA Portuguese 1469—1524	Vasco da Gama was the first explorer to sail around Africa to India. He brought back great riches from India.
FRANCISCO PIZARRO Spanish 1470—1541	Pizarro discovered and conquered the empire of the Incas in Peru. He helped build the Spanish empire in the New World.
VASCO NUÑEZ de BALBOA Spanish 1475—1517	Balboa was the first white man to see the Pacific Ocean from the shores of the New World.
FERDINAND MAGELLAN Portuguese 1480—1521	Magellan commanded the first ship ever to sail around the world. Magellan, however, died on the way.
HERNANDO CORTÉS Spanish 1485—1547	Cortés was another of the Spanish explorer-conquerors. He conquered Mexico and explored Lower California.
JACQUES CARTIER French 1491—1557	Cartier was the first explorer to sail up the St. Lawrence River. He claimed all the land near it for France.
HERNANDO de SOTO Spanish 1500—1542	De Soto explored all the southeastern part of what is now the United States. He discovered the Mississippi in his travels.
FRANCISCO CORONADO Spanish 1510—1554	Coronado explored much of what is now the United States. He discovered the Great Plains and the Grand Canyon.
SIR FRANCIS DRAKE English 1540—1596	Drake and his men were the first English explorers to sail around the world.
SIR WALTER RALEIGH English 1552—1618	Raleigh made several trips to the New World. On one of his trips he sailed up the great Orinoco River in South America.
SAMUEL de CHAMPLAIN French 1567—1635	Champlain discovered the beautiful lake we call Lake Champlain. He also founded the city of Quebec.
HENRY HUDSON English ? —1611	Hudson tried to find a northern route to China and India. He failed. But he found the Hudson River and Hudson Bay.
ABEL TASMAN Dutch 1603—1659	Tasman sailed all the way around Australia. He discovered the island which we now call Tasmania.
JACQUES MARQUETTE French 1637—1675 **LOUIS JOLIET** Canadian 1645—1700	Marquette and Joliet did much of their exploring together. They explored the Great Lakes region of North America. They also traveled for hundreds of miles down the Mississippi. Marquette was a missionary.
ROBERT CAVELIER, SIEUR de LA SALLE French 1643—1687	La Salle explored the Mississippi. He was the first person to sail all the way to its mouth.
VITUS BERING Danish 1680—1741	Bering Strait, Bering Sea, and Bering Island were named for this explorer. He was in the service of Russia.

Leif the Lucky

Columbus

Pizarro

Drake

Cook

Peary

Cousteau

Cernan

EXPLORER Nationality and Dates	EXPLORATION
JAMES COOK English 1728—1779	Captain Cook explored the South Pacific. He reached Australia and also discovered the Hawaiian Islands.
MERIWETHER LEWIS American 1774—1809 **WILLIAM CLARK** American 1770—1838	Lewis and Clark together explored much of the western half of the United States. They traveled up the Missouri River for nearly 2,000 miles. They crossed the Rockies and reached the Pacific. Their trip is called the Lewis and Clark Expedition.
DAVID LIVINGSTONE Scottish 1813—1873	Livingstone explored Africa and was missing for a long time. The journalist-explorer Henry Morton Stanley found him.
ROBERT PEARY American 1856—1920	Admiral Peary discovered the North Pole. He was the first person to reach either pole.
FRIDTJOF NANSEN Norwegian 1861—1930	Nansen sailed farther north than anyone else had ever sailed. He made this voyage before Peary had reached the Pole.
ROBERT SCOTT English 1868—1912	Scott made two trips to the Antarctic. He finally reached the South Pole, only to find that Amundsen had already been there. He and all his companions died on the return trip.
ROALD AMUNDSEN Norwegian 1872—1928	In 1911 Amundsen discovered the South Pole. Fifteen years later he flew over the North Pole.
SIR ERNEST SHACKLETON Irish 1874—1922	Shackleton explored the region near the South Pole. He made a trip with Scott on Scott's first expedition to Antarctica. Later he led two expeditions of his own.
VILHJALMUR STEFANSSON Canadian 1879—1962	Stefansson explored the Far North, and spent several whole winters there. He thought of the Arctic as a friendly place.
AUGUSTE PICCARD Swiss 1884—1962 **JACQUES PICCARD** Swiss 1922—	Auguste Piccard set a record for manned balloon flight in 1932. He and his son Jacques invented the bathyscaphe in which in 1960 Jacques set a record by descending to 7 miles below the surface of the Pacific.
RICHARD BYRD American 1888—1957	Byrd flew over the North Pole in 1926. He flew over the South Pole in 1929. He led several expeditions to Antarctica.
SIR VIVIAN FUCHS English 1908—	In 1958 Fuchs became the first explorer to cross the 2,000-mile-wide continent of Antarctica.
JACQUES-YVES COUSTEAU French 1910—	In 1963 Cousteau, already famous as an undersea explorer, set up in the Red Sea the first experimental sea-bottom colony. He shot a spectacular film of the underwater world.
SIR EDMUND HILLARY New Zealander 1919—	Hillary and Tenzing Norkay reached the top of Mt. Everest in 1953. In 1958 Hillary led an expedition to the South Pole.
WILLIAM R. ANDERSON American 1921—	In 1958 Anderson took the atomic submarine "Nautilus" across the North Pole by traveling under the polar ice.
JOHN GLENN, JR. American 1921—	Glenn was the first American astronaut to orbit the earth. In 1962 he circled the earth three times in Friendship 7.
SCOTT CARPENTER American 1925—	Astronaut Carpenter, who orbited the earth three times in Aurora 7 in 1962, in 1965 lived underwater for 30 days in Sealab II as an aquanaut.
YURI GAGARIN Russian 1934—1968	Gagarin was the first person to orbit the earth in a space capsule. He made his historic trip in 1961 in Vostok I.
EUGENE CERNAN American 1934—	Cernan, one of the astronauts aboard Gemini 9, left the spacecraft and "walked" in space for about two hours. In this time he traveled more than once around the earth.

EXPLOSIVES Gunpowder was one of the first explosives. The invention of gunpowder brought about great changes in the world. It brought about the end of the days of the robber barons and the beginning of strong nations. Ever since gunpowder was first used in war, people have worked to find better and better explosives.

But no one should think that explosives are only for war. Mining coal, building tunnels, and clearing land are a few kinds of work in which explosives are important. A series of small explosions, moreover, makes a gasoline engine run. The explosive used is a mixture of air and gasoline.

Often an explosion is caused by very rapid burning. The gases formed expand outward with great force. But sometimes in an explosion a compound is merely jarred apart. Nitrogen iodide, for instance, can be made to explode by the touch of a feather. In a nuclear explosion it is the splitting or fusing of the nuclei of atoms that is the cause.

Many explosives contain nitrogen. Nitrogen is not a good joiner. When it has joined other materials, it may readily break away and cause an explosion.

Dynamite and TNT are explosives most people have heard about. They are the ones most often used for peaceful purposes. In some places nuclear explosives, which are far more powerful, are put to use. (See ATOMS; COMPOUNDS; WEAPONS.)

EYE The diagram shows how a person's eye is built. Light enters through the transparent cornea and the opening called the pupil. The pupil is the round black spot one sees in the center of the colored part of the eye. Just back of the pupil there is a lens. This lens throws a picture on the retina at the back of the eyeball. The optic nerve goes from the retina to the brain. Whenever a picture is thrown on the retina, this nerve carries a message to the person's brain, and he sees.

The colored part, or iris, of the eye is a curtain of muscles that make the pupil larger or smaller. In bright light the pupil gets smaller. In dim light it gets larger to let more light into the eye.

The cornea must be kept moist and clean. The eyelids help keep it so by closing some 25 times a minute and washing it with liquid from the tear glands. The eyelids also shut out light during sleep. The eyelashes and eyebrows help keep out dust.

Many animals have eyes much like ours. But some animals have much simpler eyes. And some have no eyes at all. The simplest eyes are groups of sensitive cells that can only tell light from dark.

Among the most remarkable eyes are those of the dragonfly. This insect has compound eyes made up of tiny eyes. Almost all insects have compound eyes, but the dragonfly has an especially large number of little eyes in each of its compound eyes. It may have more than 30,000! (See CAMERA; CATS; LENS; LIGHT.)

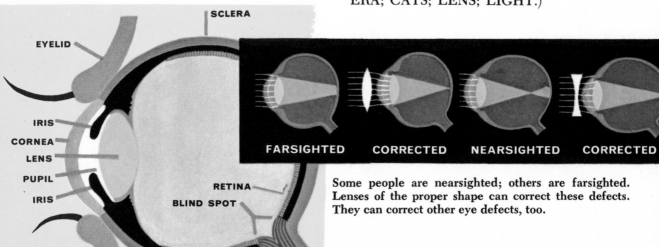

FARSIGHTED   CORRECTED   NEARSIGHTED   CORRECTED

Some people are nearsighted; others are farsighted. Lenses of the proper shape can correct these defects. They can correct other eye defects, too.

EYELID · SCLERA · IRIS · CORNEA · LENS · PUPIL · IRIS · RETINA · BLIND SPOT · EYELID · OPTIC NERVE

The letter *F* is one of five letters that can be traced back to a single letter in the Phoenician alphabet, Y. The letter came in the beginning from a picture of a nail or hook, —o. The Greeks wrote it much as we write it today: ⋏. It had the sound of *w*. The sound disappeared from their language and they gave up the sign as a letter, but they kept it to stand for the numeral 6. They called it *digamma*, because it was like two G's, Γ, or *gammas*, one on top of the other. When the Romans needed a sign for the *f* sound, they borrowed the *digamma*.

The letter *F* stands for two different sounds in English words. It has one sound in *of* and another in *four* and *five*.

FABLES A fable is a short story made up to teach a lesson. Most fables are about animals. In them animals talk.

Some fables are centuries old. Three very old ones are "The Hare and the Tortoise," "The Shepherd Boy and the Wolf," and "The Fox and the Grapes."

Many of our common sayings come from fables. "Sour grapes" is one of them. It comes from the fable "The Fox and the Grapes." In the story a fox saw a bunch of grapes hanging from a vine. They looked ripe and good to eat. But they were rather high. He jumped and jumped, but he could not reach them. At last he gave up. As he went away he said, "Those grapes were sour anyway." Now we say, "Sour grapes!" when someone pretends he does not want something he tried to get but couldn't.

Today writers do not write many fables. Comic strips and animated cartoons are taking their place. (See AESOP.)

FABRE, JEAN HENRI (1823–1915) Even before he was old enough to go to school Jean Henri Fabre was interested in insects. He thought them more fun than the cats and dogs and rabbits other children had as pets. Even as an old man he would still sit for hours watching an ant nest or a hive of bees. His neighbors thought that he was odd. But by his patient watching Fabre learned so much about insects that he became very famous.

Fabre was born in the French village of St. Léons. His family had very little money. When he was old enough, the boy peddled lemons. Later he worked on a railroad. In school he studied hard and was such a good student that he was given a college scholarship. He finished college and began teaching science when he was only 19. After nearly 30 years he gave up teaching so that he would have more time to study insects. He wrote many books about them. *The Hunting Wasps* and *The Life of the Grasshopper* are two of his books.

Fabre would have liked to go to other countries to study the insects there. But he could not afford to do so. He contented himself with studying those close at hand, and writing charming accounts of them.

No one paid much attention to Fabre's work until he was nearly 80. Then he was much honored. A few years before he died the French government gave him a pension as a reward for what he had done to aid science. (See INSECTS.)

FACTORY A great many of the things we buy today are made in factories. So many things are factory-made that handmade articles are often thought of as a luxury. It is still possible to have a pair of shoes made by hand by a cobbler. But the shoes in today's shoe stores are made in factories. It is still possible to buy handwoven cloth, but today most cloth is woven on big machines in textile mills. The same thing is true of many other articles.

A few figures tell the story of how important factories are in the United States. More than 19,000,000 men and women work in them. The workers' wages and salaries amount to more than a hundred billion dollars a year. The value of the goods manufactured runs much further into the billions. Britain, Canada, West Germany, and Japan are among the other countries that produce enormous amounts of factory goods.

Factories are rather new to the world. Up till about 200 years ago almost everything was made at home. Most workmen owned the tools they worked with. Then the steam engine was invented and, one by one, machines were made which used this new power. Factories began to spring up where workers and machines could be brought together.

The first factories were in England. They spread from there to other parts of the world. The first factory in the United States was a cotton mill. Soon after the American Revolution it was set up in Rhode Island by Samuel Slater. His machines were driven by waterpower.

Early factories were rather dismal places. The workmen worked long hours. Even children were hired for some factory work —Samuel Slater had mostly child workers. The rooms were likely to be badly lighted. In some factories there was great danger of being hurt by the machines. Not much was done for the workers' welfare.

Now factories are very different. The working hours are shorter. In most countries there are laws against hiring children for factory work. A great deal is done to safeguard the health of the workers. There are pleasant lunchrooms and, in many cases, recreation rooms.

Factories have had much to do with the growth of cities. Whole sections of many cities are given over to factories. The factory sections of cities used to be ugly and smoky. No one had the idea that a factory building could be attractive. But today good architects are hired to plan factories. Some of today's factories have lawns or even parks and playgrounds around them. Many are in suburban areas. The use of electric power instead of steam in factories does away with the need for tall smokestacks and reduces air pollution.

There is bound to be an unpleasant side to working in a factory. A workman does the same job over and over again. But factory workers can take pride in knowing that they are helping to produce many kinds of things that people could not afford if handmade. Many machines in factories are now automatic. It takes fewer and fewer workers to produce the same amount of goods. (See COMPUTER; FORD, HENRY; INDUSTRIAL REVOLUTION; MACHINERY.)

FAIRIES AND FAIRY TALES No one knows how the idea of fairies came about. But it is easy to guess. People saw things happening that they could not understand. "Some little creatures we cannot see must be at work," they said to themselves. "They must come out of hiding only at night," they argued. "And they must be very tiny or we would hear them."

The idea of tiny, invisible creatures with magic powers did not spring up in just one part of the world. It has been found in almost every part. There are ever so many stories about fairies.

In English fairy stories the fairies have a king and queen. The king is Oberon. The queen is Titania. Scandinavians have stories of a kingdom of trolls, dwarfs that lived deep in the mountains.

Some fairy stories tell of fairies that are connected with certain kinds of work or with households. The leprechauns of Ireland were supposed to be tiny shoemakers and also to be the guardians of crocks of gold. The elves in *The Elves and the Shoemaker* were experts at making shoes, too. In England brownies were said to help during the night with household tasks such as churning. Gnomes, pixies, and goblins were other tiny creatures that supposedly liked to live near people.

Puck, shown in the picture, is a fairy in Shakespeare's *A Midsummer Night's Dream.* The first book of fairy stories for children was published in 1697, long after Shakespeare's time. *Cinderella* was in that book. In that story, you remember, there is a fairy godmother. Another fairy story, *The Sleeping Beauty,* makes it clear that not all fairies are good. A wicked fairy decreed that the princess should prick her finger and fall into a deep sleep that would last till she was rescued by a prince.

Not all so-called fairy stories have fairies in them. *Little Red Riding-Hood,* for instance, is a fairy story without fairies. Any story may be called a fairy story if impossible things happen in it.

Sleeping Beauty

King of the Dwarfs

Puck

Brownies

Little Red Riding Hood

Fairy Godmother

FAIRS Trade as we know it today had its beginnings during the Middle Ages. Great fairs were the life of trade in those days. The lords allowed markets to be held in the courtyards of their castles. Peddlers carried their wares from door to door. Ironsmiths and other such workers had small shops in which they sold their wares. Churches permitted buying and selling to go on in their churchyards. But without fairs there would have been very little trade with places far away. Their growth was due partly to Charlemagne, who had urged people throughout his empire to hold markets.

Great fairs were held each year in certain cities. The fairs at London and Stourbridge in England, at Paris and Lyons in France, at Bruges and Lille in Flanders, at Frankfurt, Leipzig, and Cologne in Germany, at Geneva in Switzerland, and at Nizhni Novgorod in Russia were some of the most famous. Here spices from Arabia, silks from China, cloth from Flanders, wines from France, and furs from Russia were for sale along with many other things.

The big fairs were held every year or even several times a year, but they were not all held at the same time. Merchants traveled from one to another. As a rule a fair lasted for several weeks. Many fairs were held at the time of religious festivals, or feast days. The word fair comes from a Latin word for feast.

The fairs were often very gay. Acrobats, jugglers, dancers, and fortune-tellers made going to a fair great fun. Many of the people at every fair came for the merrymaking. "Come to the fair" was an invitation to break the dullness of ordinary days in the Middle Ages with a day of gaiety.

Fairs lost their importance late in the Middle Ages when many ocean trade routes were set up. Then trade with other lands shifted to the port cities.

Although fairs do not have the same importance they once had, many fairs are still held. In the United States many trade fairs, or exhibitions, are held regularly by people in different industries. There manufacturers show their products to prospective buyers. Only people concerned in some way with the industry attend. Many annual state and county fairs, too, are held in the United States. These fairs are held mostly to encourage farmers, stock raisers, and homemakers. Judging stock, grain, dairy products, jellies, jams, and homemade cakes is an important part of every fair. Local 4-H clubs show their accomplishments. Often schools have exhibits.

State and county fairs are part carnival. Merry-go-rounds, Ferris wheels, sideshows, and races help everyone have a good time. There is much shouting by those who have balloons, trinkets, and food to sell.

These fairs have permanent buildings. They are held in the same buildings year after year.

In 1851 a world's fair was held at London in a wonderful building called the Crystal Palace. Many countries sent exhibits to show what progress they were making in science, art, and industry. Among those the United States exhibited were false teeth, chewing tobacco, and the McCormick reaper. Since then many world's fairs have been held. The following list names some of the biggest.

1876	Centennial Exposition, Philadelphia
1889	Universal Exposition, Paris
1893	World's Columbian Exposition, Chicago
1901	Pan-American Exposition, Buffalo
1904	Louisiana Purchase Exposition, St. Louis
1905	Lewis and Clark Centennial Exposition, Portland
1909–10	Alaska-Yukon-Pacific Exposition, Seattle
1915	Panama-Pacific Internat'l Exposition, San Francisco
1924–25	British Empire Exposition, Wembley, England
1933–34	Century of Progress, Chicago
1939–40	New York World's Fair, New York
1939–40	Golden Gate Internat'l Exposition, San Francisco
1951	Festival of Britain, London
1958	Brussels World's Fair, Brussels
1962	Century 21 Exposition, Seattle
1964–65	New York World's Fair, New York
1967	Expo 67, Montreal

FAMILY LIFE A male sunfish hollows out a nest in the sand at the bottom of a lake. His mate lays her eggs there and goes away. He guards the eggs until they hatch. Then he leaves the baby fish to look out for themselves. There is no family life among the sunfish.

There *is* family life among many animals. A male robin, for instance, brings food to his mate while she is sitting on her eggs. He helps her feed the nestlings until they are strong enough to leave the nest. A male gorilla stands guard at the foot of the tree in which his mate and their young are sleeping.

In such animal families the young are fed and protected. In human families, too, the children are fed and protected. But much more is also done for them. The children are taught how to act toward other people. The manners and customs and beliefs of their society are handed down to them. The rules of the family are the only government a little child knows.

Customs are not the same the world over. Family life in different places differs in many ways. A Bedouin boy, for instance,

is taught that it would be disrespectful to eat in his father's presence. To an American child this idea would seem strange. There are many other such differences between the customs of different lands.

In very early times two ideas about families grew up. One was that the mother was the head of the family. The other was that the father was the head. The second idea became the common one. In ancient times the rule of a father over his family was often harsh. A father might even put his child to death.

In the American family the father and mother usually share the running of the home and care of the children. In some cases both the father and the mother work to earn a living for themselves and their children. Schools, churches, camps, and clubs help to do some of the training of older children that used to be done in the home by the parents.

In America the whole family often works together and plays together. A family going on a picnic is a common sight. Probably never in the past have families had so much fun together as they have today.

FARADAY, MICHAEL (1791–1867) Before the time of Michael Faraday the only way of producing electric current was by means of electric batteries. The current from batteries was not very powerful—not nearly powerful enough for most of the uses of electricity today.

In 1831 Faraday made a great discovery. For ten years or so he had had the idea that magnets could be used in getting an electric current. Now he discovered that his idea was right. He built the first electric generator, or dynamo. In this first generator a copper disk was turned between the poles of a U-shaped magnet. A coil of wire soon took the place of the copper disk. And it was found that the current can be made more powerful simply by using more turns of wire in the coil and by using more powerful magnets. The generators which supply our modern world with electricity are made of magnets and coils of wire. Water wheels or steam engines are used to run them.

Inventing the generator was Faraday's most important accomplishment, but he made many other discoveries about electricity. He made discoveries in the field of chemistry, too. Among them was benzene, the starting point in the manufacture of many dyes, perfumes, and explosives.

Faraday's accomplishments seem more wonderful when we realize that he had very little schooling. He was born in 1791 in Newington, now a part of London. His father, a blacksmith, was too poor to send him to school. So the boy went to work in a bookbinder's shop, where he became interested in books on science.

One day young Faraday attended a lecture given by a famous scientist, Sir Humphry Davy. Faraday took very careful notes at the lecture. Back at the bookshop he made diagrams to illustrate what Davy had said. Then he bound the notes and diagrams into a book and sent them to the great scientist. He wrote Davy of his interest in science and asked for work.

Faraday received the thrill of his life when, on the day before Christmas in 1812, a messenger came to the bookshop with a note asking him to call on Davy the next day. As a result of this visit Faraday became an assistant in the laboratory of this great scientist. At first Faraday only washed chemistry glassware and kept the laboratory clean, but later he was given more important work to do. It was in Davy's laboratory that Faraday received the training that enabled him to become one of the great scientists of all time. (See ELECTRICITY; ENGINES, HEAT; MAGNETS.)

Faraday's Dynamo

FAR EAST China, India, the other countries of eastern Asia, and the islands nearby are often called the Far East. Before the days of easy travel, these lands seemed very far away to the people of Europe. In Marco Polo's time it took a journey of many months to reach China by traveling eastward from Italy. From the United States the Far East is usually reached by traveling westward across the Pacific.

Columbus was one of the first explorers to think that he could reach the Far East by traveling west. His idea was good, but the Americas were in his way.

In the days of Columbus the Far East meant spices, silks, and jewels to the people of Europe. It meant strange people with strange customs. Today the people no longer seem strange. And their tin, oil, rubber, and tea are far more important to us than their spices, silks, and jewels.

Another name for the Far East is the Orient. The word "Orient" comes from the Latin word for "rising." The east is the direction of the rising sun.

FARMING For many thousands of years people had to hunt for their food. They killed wild animals and gathered roots, leaves, seeds, and the fruits of wild plants. One of the most important discoveries in the history of the world was that plants can be raised from seeds.

This discovery was made at different times in different places. In the Near East it was made some 8,000 or 10,000 years ago, back in the time called the New Stone Age. No one knows how it came about. Perhaps some seeds stored to be eaten later were accidentally covered with mud so that they sprouted. At any rate, the discovery brought about great changes in people's lives. They could now give up a life of wandering from place to place to find food. Farming was a much surer way of getting food than hunting.

Another name for farming is agriculture. "Agriculture" comes from two Latin words meaning "field" and "till." Farming is tilling the fields.

At first farmers probably raised plants only for food. But in time they began to raise them for other purposes as well. From flax they could weave linen. They learned, too, to raise cotton and to weave cloth from it. These early farmers also learned to raise animals as well as plants. Long before men were able to write records, farmers were raising sheep, cattle, goats, pigs, and donkeys.

Early Man Plowing

The first farmers had only crooked sticks for stirring up the soil. They had only stone tools and sticks for harvesting their crops. In some parts of the world farming is still very much as it was several thousand years ago. But in the United States and in most other places, too, the ways of farming are very different from the early ways. Machines of many kinds now help make the work of farmers easier.

Even modern ways of farming differ in different parts of the world. A farmer in China or the Philippines, for example, does not raise rice in the same way that a farmer in Brazil or Texas raises it. And in some lands many or all of the farms are large government-controlled enterprises rather than privately managed farms like those in the United States.

Millions of acres of farmland have been ruined by bad farming. But millions of acres that were once useless for farming have been turned into good farmland by draining swamps and by irrigation.

Today in the United States alone more than a billion acres of land are in farms. Farms are of many different kinds. On some are raised such crops as corn, wheat, rice, and cotton. There are stock farms where livestock and food for livestock are raised. Hay is likely to be one of the big crops on such farms. There are poultry farms, dairy farms, fruit farms, and small vegetable farms called truck farms.

Sizes of farms differ greatly. Farms in the United States average about 350 acres. Of course, many are smaller, but some have thousands of acres in them. In Japan the average size is just 2½ acres. More than half the farms are smaller.

The invention of farm machinery has meant that fewer farmers are needed. Better plant and animal varieties have made it possible to produce more on the same number of acres. A farmer in Illinois, for instance, used to be well pleased if he got 60 bushels of corn from an acre. Now the average is more than 90 bushels.

A farm in the United States is a pleasant place to live. Electricity helps with much of the farm work. Radio, television, telephones, and automobiles keep even farm families living in places many miles from any town in close touch with other people.

Most of the work on a farm must be done during daylight. As a rule farmers get up early in the morning. On a big farm there is work even for the children in the family. There are chickens to be fed, eggs to be gathered, vegetables to be picked, and weeds to be pulled.

The work on a farm differs with the seasons. Even in cold weather there is much to do. Machines must be gone over and repaired, sheds put in good order, and fences mended. Stock must be cared for.

A farmer, if he is to be a good one, has to know a great deal. He must be able to choose crops that are right for the soil on his farm and for the climate in which he lives. He must know how to select good seed and how to plant, care for, and harvest his crops. He must know how to fight plant diseases and insect pests. He must know how to take care of his farm animals and his farm machinery. He must know how to keep his soil from being worn out or washed away. He must know how to market what he raises. Farming has become a science. Agricultural colleges teach the science of farming and try out new ideas.

Farmers have one enemy they can do little about—bad weather. A field of oats ready for harvest may be blown down in a thunderstorm. A long stretch of dry weather may ruin the pastures on a stock farm. A severe winter may kill winter wheat and fruit trees. On the other hand, unusually good weather can be a wonderful help to farmers. A week of dry, sunshiny weather at wheat-harvesting time is "million dollar weather" to wheat farmers.

Almost all of us depend on farmers for our food. Almost all the food in our grocery stores and the meat in our meat markets come from farms in some part of the world. Without farms there could be no cities. Our farms make civilization as we know it possible. (See CROP ROTATION; DAIRYING; RANCHES.)

Plow

Sickle

Rake

McCormick Reaper

Flail

FARM MACHINERY Fifty years ago about a third of all the people in the United States lived on farms. Before that, farm families made up an even larger part of the population. Now less than one-sixteenth of the American people live on farms. But the crops are much bigger than they were 50 years ago. A farmer can produce far more in a given time than he used to. In the early 1900's every bushel of wheat a farmer raised took about 30 minutes. Now the time has gone down to a little more than 5 minutes. The amount of time needed to raise other crops has gone down, too. Better farm machinery is the reason why.

Farmers have used tools and machines for thousands of years. Rakes and plows and scythes were made very long ago. But early farming devices were simple. They were worked by hand. It was a big step upward when farmers learned to use horses and oxen to pull their farm machines. And in the 1800's many new farm machines were invented. The reaper invented by Cyrus McCormick was an important one.

After steam engines became common they were used to run some farm machinery. A steam engine pulling a threshing machine was a common sight on country roads 50 years ago. The steam engine also supplied the power for the machine after it reached the wheat or oat field.

Gradually horses and steam engines gave way to gasoline tractors. A great deal of the work done on farms today is done by tractor-drawn machinery or attachments and by big self-propelled machines. Of course, a tractor or self-propelled machine cannot work all by itself. A man has to run it and manage its controls.

The pictures show some big farm machines. Not all farms would have the same machines. An Alberta wheat grower, for instance, would have no use for a cotton picker. And a truck farmer would not need a hay baler.

The machines pictured are all used in the fields. Inside farm buildings there may be many other machines. Electricity has been brought to many farms. It helps to run indoor machines. Milking machines, pumps, crop driers, and feed-mixing machines are some. Besides, there are many machines that make housework easy for farmers' wives just as they do for housewives in towns and cities. (See DAIRYING; FARMING; INVENTIONS; WHEAT.)

Combine

Plow

Corn Picker

Forage Harvester

FASCISM (FASH izm) There are different kinds of government. When World War II began, Italy had the kind called fascism. Mussolini was the Fascist leader.

In ancient Rome the rulers had attendants each of whom carried a bundle of rods from which an ax protruded. The name for such a bundle was *fasces.* The *fasces* stood for the ruler's right to beat or cut off the heads of unruly subjects. The name fascism comes from *fasces.*

Fascists believe that the government should be very powerful. They think that a person has no rights of his own. Under fascism people are not free to write and say what they think. The government tells them what property they may own, what work they must do, and what their wages are to be. Their country must come ahead of everything else. Fascism is very different from democracy. (See DICTATORS.)

FATES Three of the Greek goddesses were called the Fates. One of them spun a thread. Her name was Clotho. The second one, Lachesis, stretched the thread out as long as she pleased. The third one, Atropos, snipped it off.

The thread was supposed to be human life. The three Fates, then, decided when a person was to be born, how long he would live, and when he would die. Not even the king of the gods, the old Greek myths said, could make the Fates change their minds. (See GREEK MYTHS.)

FBI These letters stand for Federal Bureau of Investigation. The bureau is a part of the United States government. In it there are thousands of workers.

If someone commits a crime against the United States, the FBI tries to find out who the criminal is. It has solved many puzzling cases. The stories of some of these cases are just as thrilling as any made-up detective stories.

But the FBI does much more than try to solve crimes after they are committed. It tries to prevent crime. Guarding against spies is an important part of the work of the FBI. Helping the government hire workers who will be loyal is another important task.

The FBI helps states and cities fight crime, too. One FBI file is especially helpful. This is the fingerprint file. In it are the fingerprints of every known criminal in the country. The FBI gets fingerprints from many other countries, too.

FBI agents have a nickname. It is "G-men," short for "government men." G-men do not wear uniforms.

As soon as he joins the FBI, a new agent begins a period of training. He learns what the duties of an FBI man are and how to sort out and follow up clues. He also learns how to defend himself. He must be able to shoot with either hand and be able to handle a pistol, a rifle, a shotgun, and a submachine gun. He also must learn how to use jujitsu.

There are strict rules for FBI agents. These words of J. Edgar Hoover, for over 40 years the head of the FBI, explain why: "One man didn't build the FBI, but one man can tear it down." (See FINGERPRINTS.)

FENCING For many centuries fighting a duel with swords was a common way of settling an argument. Many men were killed in such duels. About 600 years ago, to better defend themselves in duels, men began practicing the use of the sword with skilled fencing masters. The game of fencing grew out of such practicing.

In fencing, the ends of the swords are blunted and the players are masked. A touch is counted as a wound. Three kinds of swords are used. The swords are for different types of fencing. The foil is a slender, flexible, and pointed sword. The touch must be made with the point on the trunk of the body. The épée (AY PAY), or dueling sword, is stiffer. The touch must be with the point, but it may be made on any part of the body. The saber has a heavier blade. Touches are scored with the point or edge on any part of the body except the legs. (See GAMES AND SPORTS; OLYMPIC GAMES.)

Christmas Fern

Venus Maidenhair Fern

Climbing Fern

Grape Fern

Long Beech Fern

Maidenhair Fern

Rattlesnake Fern

Purple Cliff Brake

FERNS Millions of years before there were any flowering plants on the earth there were ferns. There were a great many ferns in the ancient forests from which coal was made. Some of these ferns were as big as trees. Today there are very few ferns compared with the number of flowering plants, and really large ferns grow only in the tropics. Most of the ferns of cooler lands grow in moist, shady woods.

Ferns do not grow from seeds. They grow from spores instead. The spores are formed in little brown spore cases which are often found on the underside of the leaves. Sometimes the spore cases are produced on special stalks instead. The spores are very tiny and are easily carried about by the wind. When they fall in a place where light and moisture conditions are right, they begin to grow.

Strangely enough, these spores do not produce other fern plants like the fern plants they come from. Instead, they grow into flat, ribbon- or heart-shaped plants that are about the size of a man's thumbnail. These plants are so small that not many people ever notice them.

The small "thumbnail" plants in turn produce fern plants of the kinds we are used to seeing. Thus new fern plants do not look like their parents; they look like their grandparents.

The ferns we see have roots, stems, and leaves just as flowering plants have. The stem of a fern, however, is usually under the ground. Buds on the stem produce the leaves, which grow upward through the ground. A young fern leaf is wound up into a coil. As the leaf grows, the coil unwinds. Because a coiled leaf looks like the scroll at the head of a violin, young fern leaves are often called fiddleheads. The veins in fern leaves have a special way of branching. Each one, when it divides, forks into two equal branches.

There are many different kinds of ferns. Some of them do not look at all like the ferns we know best. But they show they are ferns by their spore cases, by their fiddleheads, and by the way their veins fork. (See COAL; PLANT KINGDOM.)

FIBERS The skins of animals made warm clothing for our early ancestors. There was no other material they could use. But in time people found that they could make certain threadlike fibers into cloth. Some of these fibers they got from animals. Some they got from plants. For thousands of years people have made linen cloth from fibers in the stem of the flax plant and cotton cloth from the fibers on cotton seeds. They have made woolen cloth from the wool of sheep and silk cloth from the fibers in the cocoon of the silkworm.

One by one other fibers came into use. Among the other plant fibers are jute, hemp, ramie, kapok, sisal, and palm. Among the other animals that furnish fibers are the camel, yak, alpaca, goat, rabbit, and pig. Besides, there are now many man-made, or synthetic, fibers. They are manufactured from such things as coal, petroleum, wood, and milk. Rayon, nylon, and dacron are three of the best known.

We use fibers for many things besides cloth. Twine, rope, carpets, brushes, paper, and stuffing for mattresses are a few of their many uses. (See COTTON; LINEN; NYLON; RAYON; SILK; WOOL.)

FIELD, EUGENE (1850–1895) "Little Boy Blue" is a poem many people love. It is the most famous of the poems for children written by Eugene Field. Another well-known one is "Wynken, Blynken, and Nod."

Eugene Field was born in St. Louis, but he spent most of his boyhood in New England. After college he went into newspaper work and worked in several cities. All the later years of his life he was with the *Chicago Morning News*. He wrote a column called "Sharps and Flats."

Field wrote many kinds of things well— stories, essays, poems. It is no wonder that he wrote especially well for children, for he had seven children of his own. He was very fond of them. The top of his desk was almost sure to have toys on it.

Field did not live to see his children grow up. He died when he was only 45. He was so well liked that thousands of people felt that they had lost a friend. In Chicago a memorial to him shows an angel sprinkling sand in the eyes of two sleeping children to bring them pleasant dreams.

Ridges of Skin on Fingertip

FINGERPRINTS The skin on the ends of our fingers has ridges on it. These ridges show clearly through a magnifying glass. About 80 years ago an Englishman verified an amazing discovery. He found out for sure that no two people have exactly the same pattern of ridges on their fingertips. The Englishman was Sir Francis Galton.

The British government saw a way of putting this discovery to use. They began using fingerprints to track down criminals. A fingerprint is merely a record of the pattern of ridges on a person's finger. To make a fingerprint all one has to do is to press his finger on an inked pad and then on paper. In 1901 Scotland Yard of London started a file of the fingerprints of all the criminals they caught. Later, if fingerprints were found at the scene of a crime, the police could check with their fingerprint files. In many cases they found that the crime was committed by someone whose fingerprints were on record.

Fingerprints are a big help in catching criminals. They are useful in many other ways, too. Many hospitals fingerprint newborn babies so that the babies cannot get mixed up. Soldiers are fingerprinted as a way of identifying them if they are killed in action. Government workers are fingerprinted to help guard important secrets. The FBI of the United States now has millions of fingerprints on file. Among them are those of many private citizens who want their fingerprints on file in case of accident or loss of memory. (See FBI.)

FINLAND The country of Finland lies far north in Europe. Helsinki, its capital, is called the "White City of the North." It is in southernmost Finland. But no other country on any continent has a capital so far north. Helsinki is not, however, as far north as Reykjavík, the capital of Iceland.

A trip from Helsinki to Finland's northern border is about 700 miles long. That border is very near the southern ends of fiords on the Arctic coast. But those fiords are in a narrow strip of land in Norway. Finland has no Arctic coast. Its neighbors are Norway, Sweden, and the Soviet Union. It is farther from the open Atlantic than Norway and Sweden. But it has seaports on its western and southern coasts.

Finland is about half the size of Texas. Only six of Europe's more than 30 countries are bigger.

The country is not thickly settled. Much of northern Finland is in the almost empty region called Lapland, where the Lapps roam with their herds of reindeer. Most of Finland's 4,660,000 people live in the southern part of the country.

Finland is not a very good farming country, partly because it is so far north. Besides, there is not much good soil. Long ago, during the Ice Age, the ice scraped off much of the soil and carried it away. There is bare rock in places. Some land, moreover, is swampy. A little less than a tenth of all Finland's land is farmed, and most of the farms are tiny. But Finnish farmers do well with what they have. The main crops are oats, wheat, barley, hay, and potatoes. Many farms are dairy farms.

Some Finns are fishermen. Some work in the country's copper, iron, and zinc mines. But Finland's trees are its great natural wealth. There are forests on about three-fourths of its land. Many of the Finnish people get their living from the forests. Some are lumbermen. Others manufacture things of wood. Finland's chief exports are wood, wood pulp, and paper. The Finns take good care of their forests.

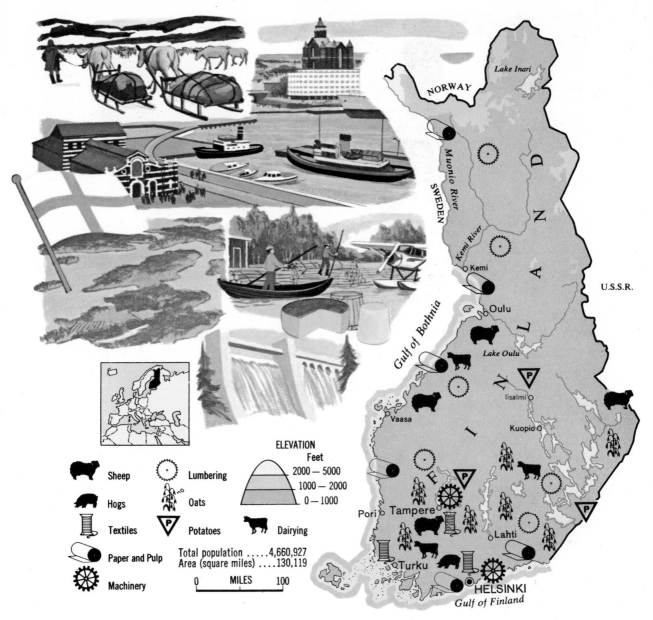

ELEVATION
Feet
2000 — 5000
1000 — 2000
0 — 1000

Sheep

Hogs

Textiles

Paper and Pulp

Machinery

Lumbering

Oats

Potatoes

Dairying

Total population 4,660,927
Area (square miles) 130,119

0 MILES 100

Finland is sometimes called a "land of a thousand lakes." Really it has more than 50 thousand. Many, joined by canals, are routes used by ships and timber rafts. There are many streams, too. Falls in some of them furnish power to run the machines of factories. Unfortunately, Finland's lakes and streams have been mostly fished out or have been ruined for fishing by wastes from the paper mills.

For years Finland was somewhat out of the way for tourists. But now Helsinki is easily reached by plane. And there are air-lines, railroads, and good roads inside Finland. Each year many tourists go to a resort on the Arctic Circle to see the midnight sun and watch thrilling lumberjack contests. Some visit Lapland villages.

Helsinki has a great stadium, built for the Olympic games of 1952. Near it is the statue of a runner, done by a Finnish sculptor. The city has fine government buildings and churches. Even its factory sections are well kept. Visitors to Finland see many signs that the Finnish people are hardworking, thrifty, and gifted.

FIORD (FYORD) A fiord is a long, narrow arm of the sea that lies in a steep-walled mountain valley. Of course, there can be fiords only where mountains come down to the edge of the sea. Waterfalls are common on the steep fiord walls.

A river of ice—a valley glacier—helped make every fiord. The river of ice gouged its valley deeper and deeper as it moved toward the sea. After the ice melted, the sea flooded the valley. Some fiords are astonishingly deep—more than 4,000 feet.

Norway is famous for its fiords. There are fiords along the coasts of Alaska, Greenland, New Zealand, and Chile, too. (See GLACIER; ICE AGE; NORWAY.)

FIRE Our caveman ancestors used fire to cook their food. They used fire to warm and light their caves. They used fire to corner animals they hunted. Early man may have used fire long before he knew how to make it himself. For lightning must frequently have started forest fires in prehistoric times just as it does now. Probably ancient hunters often carried home burning branches from such fires.

But in time man discovered ways of starting fires. The oldest ways are rubbing two dry sticks together and striking sparks from stones. Today we can start a fire easily with matches or electric sparks.

Scientists tell us that when any substance burns it unites with oxygen, one of the gases in the air. Something is always left in place of a substance that burns up. But we do not always see this something. When wood burns, for instance, the wood disappears. A few ashes are left. But most of the wood has been changed to invisible water vapor and carbon dioxide.

Think of eating all our meat raw! Of living in houses unheated in the winter! Of having no automobiles or trains or airplanes! The very suggestion makes us realize how hard it would be to get along without fire. But fire out of control is a terrible enemy. Every year it does millions of dollars' worth of damage and costs a great many lives. (See COOKING; FUELS; MATCHES; OXYGEN.)

Making Fire with Bow and Drill

FIRE FIGHTING

FIRE FIGHTING Every modern city has a fire department. Fire can do so much harm that we have worked out good ways of fighting it. Even many small villages have fire departments.

A city fire department always has both fire engines and hook-and-ladder wagons. A fire engine pumps a powerful stream of water from a hydrant. Water puts out a fire chiefly by cooling whatever is burning. Fire engines carry chemicals, too. These chemicals are better than water for fighting some kinds of fire. Water, for instance, is not good for fighting oil fires. The ladders of the hook-and-ladder wagons let firemen reach upper floors of buildings. Cities on rivers, lakes, or seas often have fireboats. These boats pump water on fires near the bank or shore.

Fighting fire in a forest is quite different from fighting fire in a city. There are no hydrants to furnish water. One way of fighting a forest fire is to clear all the trees away from a broad strip some distance in front of the fire. If the strip is wide enough, the fire will not be able to leap across it. Sometimes a trench is dug instead. Chemicals may be dropped from aircraft either on the fire itself or on the areas ahead.

When a fire starts, there may not be time to wait for a fire engine to come.

The "Joe Ross," the world's first successful steam fire engine, was first used in Cincinnati in 1853.

Courtesy of Smithsonian Institution and Insurance Company of North America

Fighting a Forest Fire

Everyone needs to know some simple ways of putting out small fires.

A good way of putting out some fires is to smother them with a heavy overcoat, blanket, or rug. When a person's clothes catch fire, the fire can often be put out quickly in this way.

Fire extinguishers are a big help, too. There are several kinds. In one kind carbon dioxide is produced. The carbon dioxide forces out a stream of water onto the fire. Some kinds of extinguishers have liquid chemicals that change to heavy gases when put on a fire. The gases shut off the air and smother the fire. There are dry-chemical extinguishers, too, that can be used to smother a fire. Still another kind of extinguisher sends out a smothering blanket of tough foam.

Of course, the very best way of fighting fires is to keep them from getting started. If no one were careless about fire, fire fighters would not have much work to do. (See CARBON DIOXIDE.)

Early Fire Fighting Tools

Early Fire Hydrant

Courtesy of Insurance Company of North America

FIREWORKS The best part of a Fourth of July celebration, many people think, is the fireworks. No Fourth would be complete without them.

Roman candles are a simple kind of fireworks. They are made in this way: The inside of a cardboard tube is divided into several separate little rooms. In the center of each room there is a hollow ball made of powder that will burn. The powder has gum and shellac mixed with it to hold it in shape. It has chemicals mixed with it to give it a pretty color when it burns. Packed around the ball there is loose powder. When the fuse is lighted and the loose powder in the first room is set on fire, the powder explodes and shoots the ball out of the tube. As the powder in room after room explodes, ball after ball comes out. The balls themselves burn after they have been shot up into the air.

There are fireworks of many other kinds. But they are all made of much the same chemicals and other materials.

Fireworks are dangerous. Most places in the United States now have laws limiting their sale. Today, instead of having fireworks in their backyards on the Fourth of July, people go to see a fireworks display at some place where there are men who can handle fireworks safely. (See EXPLOSIVES; FOURTH OF JULY; ROCKETS.)

FISHER The fisher is one of the wild animals of Canada. It belongs to the weasel family. It is, then, a cousin of the mink, the marten, the weasel, and the skunk. A male fisher is one of the biggest animals in the weasel family. The female is much smaller than the male.

This animal got its name not because it catches fish but because it sometimes steals fish from fishermen's traps. It eats chiefly such animals as squirrels, mice, and rabbits. The fisher is one of the few animals that will attack a porcupine.

Like most of its relatives, the fisher gets about wonderfully well on land. Its cousin the marten is very fast. It can run fast enough to catch a squirrel. But the fisher is even faster. It can run fast enough to catch a marten. The fisher can climb trees easily, too. And it can make 40-foot leaps from branch to branch.

A fisher's silky fur is very valuable. For years fishers have been hunted and trapped for their pelts.

A fisher makes its home in a hollow tree. Like most meat-eating animals, it does much of its hunting at night. (See BALANCE IN NATURE; FURS; MAMMALS.)

FISHES All fishes live in water. But not all animals that live in water are fish. Some animals are called fish by mistake. The starfish is not a fish. Neither are the jellyfish, the crayfish, or any of the shellfish. To be a true fish an animal must have gills, it must have fins, and it must not at any time during its life have legs. Most fishes, but not all, are covered with scales.

Gills take oxygen out of the air that is dissolved in water. Gills are thin threads or branches made of tissue. Oxygen can pass into the blood inside the gills. Most fishes are unable to breathe out of water. Lungfishes, however, have lungs, too, and can breathe with their lungs when the ponds where they live dry up.

Fins are a great help in swimming. A fish pushes itself forward by moving its tail and tail fin from side to side. Its other fins help it keep its balance. They also help guide it. Most fishes have sacs filled with air inside their bodies. These sacs are called air bladders. They are a great help in swimming upward or downward. To go down, a fish lets some air out of its air bladder. To go up, it forces more air into it.

No fishes ever have legs, although a few fishes do sometimes use their fins as legs and make short excursions out of water. The climbing perch is one.

Fishes are cold-blooded; they are the same temperature as the water around them. Some of them can become very cold without being harmed. Fish have even been frozen in blocks of ice and have been able to swim away when the ice melted.

Many fishes are meat eaters. Some eat plants. Others eat both plants and animals.

Fishes have eyes, but only a very few have eyelids. The eyes of most fishes are always open. As a rule, a fish has one eye on each side of its head. The flounder and some of its close relatives, however, swim on their sides and have both their eyes on the upper side of their heads.

Most fishes have a good sense of touch. Some have sensitive whiskers hanging from their "chins." Many have a lateral line, a line of special cells that let them feel movements in the water.

Fishes have no outer ears, but they do have ears deep in their heads. Probably, however, they cannot hear at all well.

Fishes have a keen sense of smell. In only a few cases are their nostrils useful for breathing.

At least some fishes can taste their food. A bullhead, for instance, has taste buds scattered over its skin. It can taste its food before it eats it.

A few fishes build nests and guard their eggs. But most fishes do not. Many small tropical fishes bear their young alive. The mother fish carries her eggs in her body until they develop into baby fish.

Some fishes when they are grown up have good weapons. The lion-fish is one. The stingray is another. But baby fish have no way of protecting themselves. And they are good food for bigger animals. A baby fish has very little chance of growing up. If

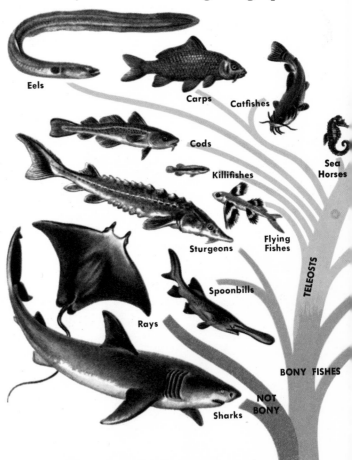

Eels

Carps　Catfishes

Cods

Killifishes

Sea Horses

Flying Fishes

Sturgeons

Spoonbills

TELEOSTS

Rays

BONY FISHES

NOT BONY

Sharks

fish as a rule did not lay a great many eggs, most fishes would soon disappear.

Altogether there are about 30,000 kinds of fishes. A great many of them have what we think of as a fish shape. But some, as you see, do not. Today's largest fish is the whale shark, which may be 50 feet long. In contrast, a goby measures half an inch.

Some of the thousands of kinds of fishes live in salt water all their lives. Some live in fresh water. And some spend part of their lives in each.

Fishes are caught by the billions for food. Tuna, whitefish, salmon, herring, mackerel, and cod are among the important food fishes. (See ELECTRIC FISHES; GAME FISHES; LUNGFISH; TROPICAL FISHES.)

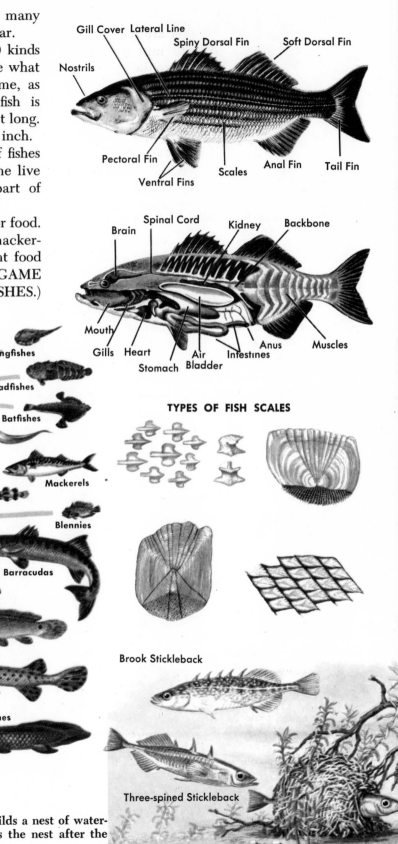

Gill Cover · Lateral Line · Spiny Dorsal Fin · Soft Dorsal Fin · Nostrils · Pectoral Fin · Ventral Fins · Scales · Anal Fin · Tail Fin

Brain · Spinal Cord · Kidney · Backbone · Mouth · Gills · Heart · Stomach · Air Bladder · Intestines · Anus · Muscles

Flounders · Filefishes · Clingfishes · Toadfishes · Batfishes · Remoras · Sea Robins · Cutlass Fishes · Mackerels · Basses · Gobies · Blennies · Mullets · Barracudas · Gouramis · Butterfishes · Pikes · Bowfin · Herrings · Gars · Coelacanths · Lungfishes

TYPES OF FISH SCALES

Brook Stickleback

Three-spined Stickleback

Female in Nest

The little stickleback builds a nest of water-weeds. The male guards the nest after the female lays eggs in it.

Fishing in Ancient Days with Spear and Trap

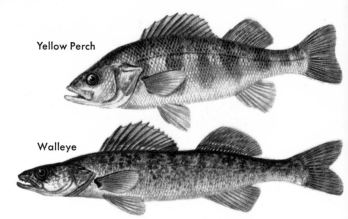

Yellow Perch

Walleye

TWO COMMON FRESHWATER FISHES

FISHING For thousands of years people have caught fish for food. Perhaps people got the idea of fishing when they saw birds diving for fish, or animals such as otters watching for fish from the banks of streams. At any rate, fishing has been an important occupation from the earliest times.

Today many people catch food for themselves by fishing. They fish mostly for the fun of it. But there is commercial fishing, too—catching fish to sell. Fishing vessels go out from lakeshores and seacoasts all over the world. Most of the catch is of food fishes to be sold fresh, dried, canned, or frozen. But many of the fish caught are used for oil and fish meal.

Certain places are especially good for fishing. The Grand Bank of Newfoundland is one of them. Here the moving waters of the sea bring in plenty of food for huge numbers of fish.

The herring is a food fish caught in enormous numbers. It is an ocean fish. Other important food fishes of the sea are cod, haddock, mackerel, tuna, and halibut. Among the important freshwater fishes are trout and whitefish. Salmon, which are caught and canned by the millions, hatch in fresh water but live most of their lives in the sea. The menhaden, an ocean fish, ranks at the top of the list of fishes caught for oil and fish meal.

Some fishes travel in big groups, or schools. At a certain place there may be a great run of a fish. Then there may be no more at that place for days.

Many stories have been written about the hardships and dangers of life on fishing vessels. With the faster, sturdier boats of today there is much less danger than there used to be.

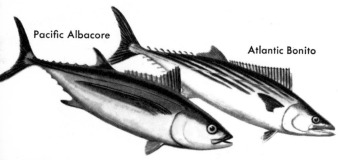

Pacific Albacore

Atlantic Bonito

Fishing for Tuna

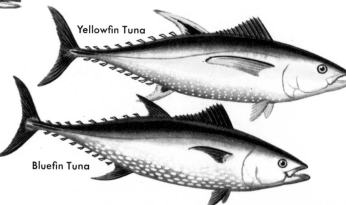

Yellowfin Tuna

Bluefin Tuna

A purse seine is set around a school of fish, then shut and partly hauled aboard to bail out the fish.

Nets of different kinds are used in commercial fishing. There is long-line fishing, too, with many hooks on one line—sometimes more than 5,000.

People who fish for themselves usually use a hook and line. They put bait on the hook. The fish swallows the hook when it eats the bait. Worms and minnows are common fish bait. Many fishermen use a rather short pole, or rod, and a line that can be wound around a reel. They may use artificial flies instead of bait to lure fish.

Probably the most famous of all people who have fished for fun is Izaak Walton. He lived in England in the 1600's. He wrote a book called *The Compleat Angler*. His name stands for good sportsmanship.

Fish are caught in such huge numbers that there is danger some kinds will disappear. To help keep their waters stocked with fish, several governments operate fish hatcheries. The young fish hatched are turned loose when they are large enough. Governments have laws to regulate fishing, too. Baby fish have so many enemies that only about one in a thousand grows up. Perhaps some such plan as netting off areas in the sea to protect the fish there will one day have to be followed if there is always to be good fishing. (See GAME FISHES.)

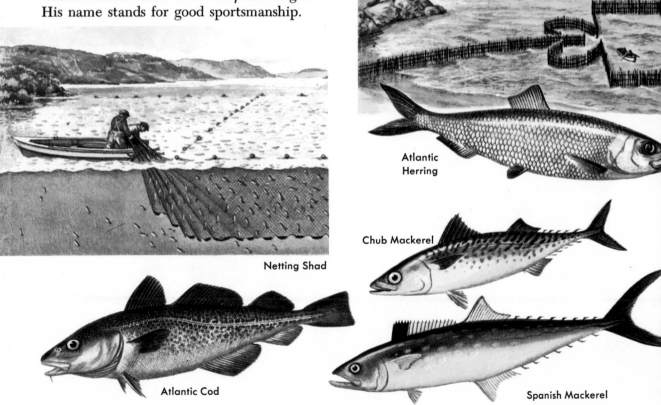

Herring Weir (Trap)

Netting Shad

Atlantic Herring

Chub Mackerel

Atlantic Cod

Spanish Mackerel

FLAG The idea of flags is ancient. When the soldiers of olden times went into battle they needed to know where their leaders were. In the confusion of the fighting it was not easy to tell. The leaders therefore formed the custom of showing where they were by carrying a tall pole of some kind. As long as soldiers could see the pole, they fought on. If it fell, they knew that their leader was lost. The pole usually had some emblem at the top. It might be a shield, or a fan of feathers, or a figure of a god or of some animal. These emblems were the forerunners of our modern flags.

The Romans were the first Europeans to use flags of cloth. Their flags were square. They were fastened to crossbars at the ends of spears. They hung down, just as many banners do today. For a long time flags were banners fastened at the upper corners to horizontal bars. The knights of the Middle Ages had flags of this kind. A knight's flag had the same decoration as his shield.

The idea of fastening flags to the side of a pole came to Europe by way of the Saracens. These Arabs went into battle with their flags fastened at the side and flying out in the breeze. "With flags flying" came to mean that everything is going well.

Flags of countries were not common until about 200 years ago. Now almost every country has its flag. The flag of the United States was one of the first to mean a great deal to the people of a whole nation.

Every flag has a meaning. The 13 stripes of the American flag stand for the 13 colonies that became the first states. In the blue square there are stars. They stand for the states now in the United States. The colors of a country's flag are not just colors chosen by chance, either. George Washington, a story tells, explained the colors of the American flag in this way: "We take the stars and blue union from heaven, the red from our mother country, separating it by white stripes, thus showing we have separated from her; and the white stripes shall go down to posterity representing liberty."

There are many rules telling how our flag should be treated. These rules make up the federal flag code. The code says that the Stars and Stripes should never touch the ground. It says that, except on special occasions and at special places, the flag should be flown only from sunrise to sunset. There are many other rules telling how the flag should be flown and handled.

One of the newer flags is that of the United Nations. Some rules of the code had to be changed when it came into use. For it stands not for one country but for all the countries in the United Nations.

All countries love their flags and often mention them in patriotic songs. The national anthem of the United States, for instance, is "The Star-Spangled Banner." (See BALTIMORE; DENMARK; OLD GLORY; PATRIOTIC SONGS.)

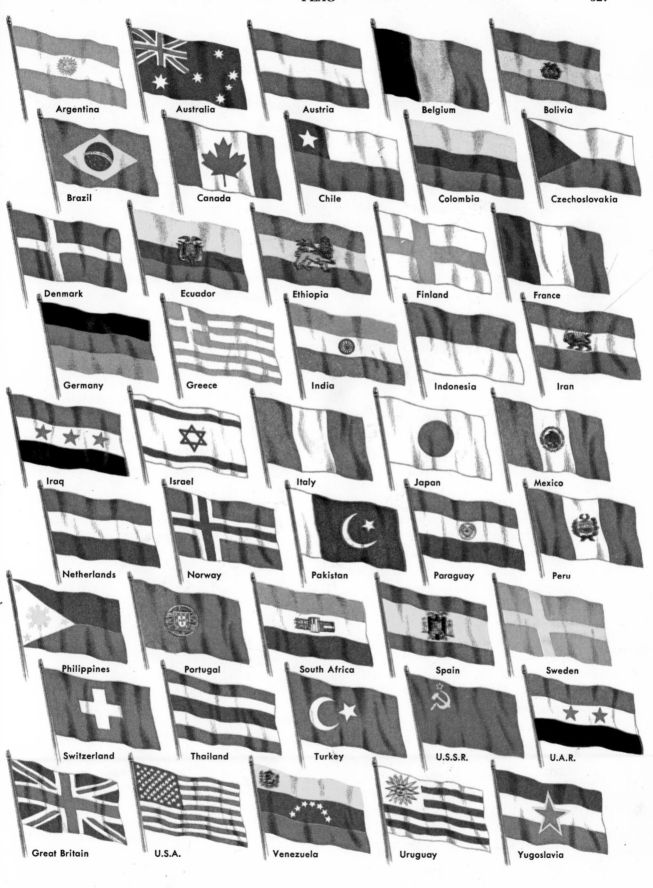

Argentina   Australia   Austria   Belgium   Bolivia

Brazil   Canada   Chile   Colombia   Czechoslovakia

Denmark   Ecuador   Ethiopia   Finland   France

Germany   Greece   India   Indonesia   Iran

Iraq   Israel   Italy   Japan   Mexico

Netherlands   Norway   Pakistan   Paraguay   Peru

Philippines   Portugal   South Africa   Spain   Sweden

Switzerland   Thailand   Turkey   U.S.S.R.   U.A.R.

Great Britain   U.S.A.   Venezuela   Uruguay   Yugoslavia

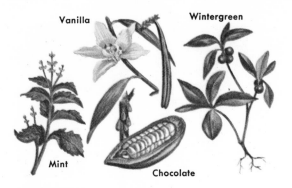

Vanilla Wintergreen Mint Chocolate

FLAVORING Candy comes in a number of different flavors. So does chewing gum. So do ice cream and puddings and many other kinds of desserts.

The most popular flavoring for ice cream and cake is vanilla. A great deal of soft candy has vanilla in it, too. Vanilla comes from the seedpods of an orchid. No one in the Old World had ever heard of vanilla until the Spaniards conquered Mexico about 400 years ago. The Spaniards learned how to make it from the Aztecs.

These Indians were also using chocolate. Chocolate is now a very popular flavoring.

Peppermint, spearmint, and wintergreen are made from the leaves of mint and wintergreen plants. They are the best-liked flavorings for chewing gum.

Peppermint and wintergreen are also used in hard candies. Many fruit flavorings are used in these candies, too. Lemon and orange flavorings are made from the rinds of lemons and oranges. Most fruit flavorings are made from fruit juices.

Actually the good taste flavorings give the things we eat is partly a good smell. There are really only four tastes—bitter, sour, sweet, and salty. Most of the rest of the taste of anything is its smell. Smell is a stronger sense than taste. If you were smelling a pear while eating an apple, the apple would taste like a pear.

At first all flavorings were made from plants. Now scientists have learned to make many in other ways. Artificial vanilla, for instance, is now made from coal tar! (See CHOCOLATE AND COCOA; COAL TAR; HERBS; SPICES.)

FLAX Linen is made of fibers from the stems of flax plants. These fibers can be made into thread that is coarse and strong or as fine as spider-web silk. The coarse threads are used for making twine and coarse linen.

The seeds of flax are useful, too. Linseed oil is made from them. This oil is used in making paint, oilcloth, linoleum, and patent leather. Linseed cake, left over when oil is pressed from flax seeds, is good feed for cattle and other animals.

There are different kinds of flax. Some are raised chiefly for their seeds. Others are grown chiefly for their fibers. Seed flax usually grows to be from 15 to 20 inches tall. Fiber flax is taller; it grows to be from 30 to 48 inches high.

Flax is grown in many countries. Among the largest producers of seed flax are Argentina, Canada, India, and the United States. In Europe flax is grown chiefly for fiber. The Soviet Union is the world's largest producer of flax fiber.

Probably the earliest use of flax was as food. Our Stone Age ancestors probably

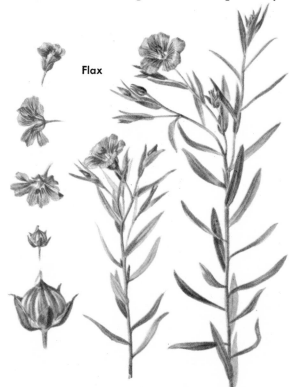

Flax

first gathered the seeds of wild flax to eat. Then they learned to cultivate it. Flax has been found in ruins of homes of the Swiss Lake Dwellers. By 5000 B.C. flax was being raised in ancient Egypt for both fiber and seed—linen and oil.

A flax plant in bloom is very pretty. Some kinds of flax are raised in flower gardens. (See LINEN; PAINT.)

FLOOD Sometimes so much water runs into a river that there is not enough room for all of it between the banks. The river spills over onto the land nearby. We say that there is a flood.

A flood may do much damage. It may carry away houses and bridges. People and animals may be drowned. Crops may be ruined, and good soil washed away.

Floods along rivers often come after a few days of warm weather in early spring. Water from melting snow runs into rivers faster than the rivers can carry it off. Floods may come, too, after several days of steady, drenching rain.

Sometimes there are floods that come all of a sudden after one very heavy rain. These are called flash floods. Usually the weatherman can warn people when a flood is coming. But he cannot give any advance warning of a flash flood.

Cutting down our forests has helped cause floods along rivers. Water can run into streams faster down bare slopes than down slopes covered with forests.

The sea may flood the land, too. A great storm at sea or an earthquake may pile up the water of the sea and make it rush in far past the shore. The breaking of dikes along coasts or riverbanks may cause disastrous floods.

China has probably suffered more than any other country from floods. In 1939, for instance, a million people were drowned and millions more were left homeless.

In 1937 the Ohio and Mississippi rivers overflowed, causing the worst flood ever known in the United States. This flood destroyed property worth nearly $500,000,000, killed 150 people, and left a million or so people without homes.

Much of the land of the Netherlands is protected by dikes since it is below the level of the sea. From time to time there have been breaks in the dikes. In 1953, for example, the sea broke through and covered thousands of acres of land. Nearly 2,000 people were drowned.

In 1966 Italy had its most disastrous widespread flood in a thousand years! The greatest damage was done to the city of Florence. Many of its priceless art treasures were ruined. (See DIKES AND LEVEES; EROSION; HWANG HO; MISSISSIPPI RIVER; NILE RIVER; U.S. WEATHER BUREAU.)

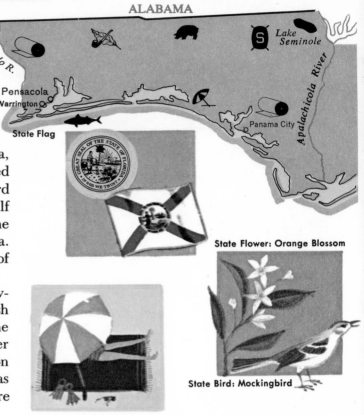

State Flag

State Flower: Orange Blossom

State Bird: Mockingbird

FLORIDA The "Sunshine State," Florida, fills all of a peninsula in southeastern United States. The peninsula reaches southward between the Atlantic Ocean and the Gulf of Mexico for 450 miles. Florida has the longest coastline of any state except Alaska. Key West, Fla., is the southernmost city of the states on the continent.

The Spanish word *florida* means "flowery." Soon after Easter in 1513 a Spanish explorer, Ponce de León, landed on the peninsula. The Spanish words for Easter mean "flowery festival." Ponce de León called the region Florida because it was Easter time and also, perhaps, because there were so many flowers there.

Since Florida is on the eastern coast, many people are surprised to find that it is not one of the original 13 states. But Florida was not a part of the United States until 1819. After 1513 the peninsula belonged first to Spain, then to England, and then to Spain again. The United States bought Florida from Spain in 1819. Florida became the 27th state in 1845. It withdrew from the Union in 1861 during the Civil War and was readmitted in 1868.

Florida is a middle-sized state. Twenty-one states are larger. But only eight have more people, and the population is growing fast. The capital is Tallahassee.

A mild climate, wide beaches, beautiful scenery, and game fish in the sea have helped to make Florida a famous resort state. Among the most popular resort cities are Miami Beach and Fort Lauderdale on the east coast and St. Petersburg and Tampa on the west coast. Many Floridians make their living from the tourist trade.

Tourists by the thousands visit St. Augustine, the oldest town in the United States.

It was founded in 1565. They visit Tarpon Springs to see the gay boats of the sponge fishermen. In the south they see the vast Everglades swampland with its alligators, birds, and almost tropical scenery.

Fruit raising and farming are important ways of earning a living in Florida, too. Groves of oranges, grapefruit, and other citrus fruits stretch across central Florida from the Atlantic to the Gulf. Acres of truck gardens lie on the coastal lands, especially those near Miami and Tampa, and in north-central Florida. Truck farmers grow such vegetables as tomatoes, celery, beans, and potatoes. On Florida's prairie land farmers raise fine beef cattle.

The number of factories and mills in Florida is growing. The most important factory work today is the freezing and canning of foods from orchards, farms, and fisheries. Frozen orange juice is one of Florida's leading products. Forests that cover more than half the state furnish mills with wood for lumber and pulpwood for paper-making. Such miscellaneous products as

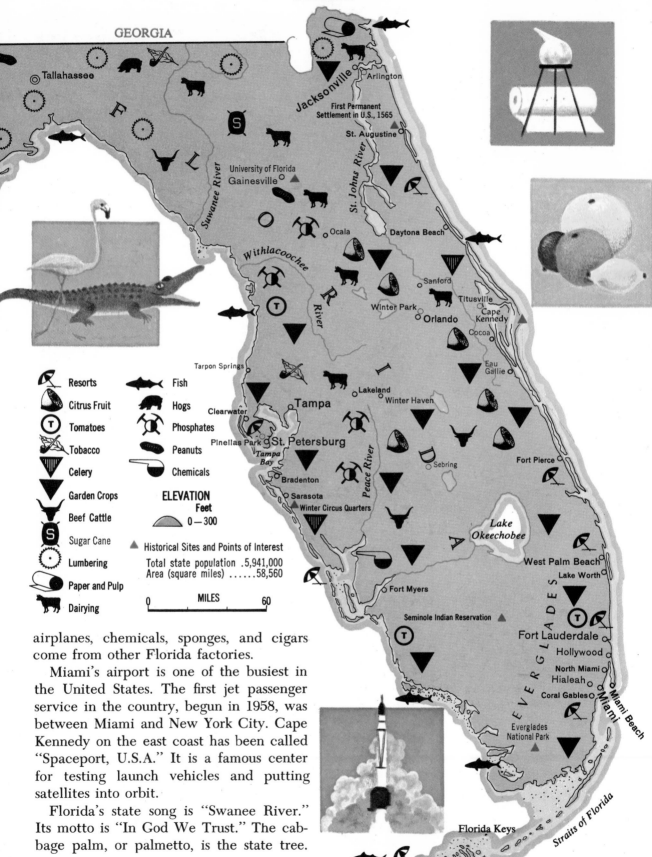

GEORGIA

Tallahassee

F O L

Suwanee River

S

Withlacoochee

River

University of Florida
Gainesville

Ocala

Jacksonville

Arlington

First Permanent
Settlement in U.S., 1565

St. Augustine

St. Johns River

Daytona Beach

Sanford

Winter Park

Orlando

Titusville
Cape
Kennedy

Cocoa

Eau
Gallie

Tarpon Springs

Clearwater

Pinellas Park

Tampa

St. Petersburg

Tampa
Bay

Bradenton

Sarasota

Winter Circus Quarters

Lakeland

Winter Haven

I

D

Sebring

A

Fort Pierce

Lake
Okeechobee

West Palm Beach
Lake Worth

Fort Myers

Seminole Indian Reservation

EVERGLADES

Fort Lauderdale

Hollywood

North Miami
Hialeah

Coral Gables

Miami
Miami Beach

Everglades
National Park

Florida Keys

Straits of Florida

Key West

Resorts

Citrus Fruit

T Tomatoes

Tobacco

Celery

Garden Crops

Beef Cattle

S Sugar Cane

Lumbering

Paper and Pulp

Dairying

Fish

Hogs

Phosphates

Peanuts

Chemicals

**ELEVATION
Feet**

0 – 300

▲ Historical Sites and Points of Interest
Total state population .5,941,000
Area (square miles) 58,560

MILES

0   60

airplanes, chemicals, sponges, and cigars
come from other Florida factories.

Miami's airport is one of the busiest in
the United States. The first jet passenger
service in the country, begun in 1958, was
between Miami and New York City. Cape
Kennedy on the east coast has been called
"Spaceport, U.S.A." It is a famous center
for testing launch vehicles and putting
satellites into orbit.

Florida's state song is "Swanee River."
Its motto is "In God We Trust." The cabbage palm, or palmetto, is the state tree.

FLOUR   Recipes for bread, cake, and cookies all call for flour. In the United States, if the recipe says simply "flour," it is sure to mean flour from wheat seeds. The seeds, or grains, are ground between rollers. The ground-up grain is then sifted to separate the fine, powdery part from the coarser part. The fine, powdery part comes mostly from the food stored up inside the seed for the baby plant. The coarser part comes mostly from the outside seed coat. Fine white flour has been rolled and sifted several times. Whole wheat flour contains almost the whole grain. It has not been rolled and sifted as many times.

There are many other kinds of flour. Most of them are made from seeds, just as wheat flour is. Among those from seeds are rye, buckwheat, and rice flours, and cornmeal. Flour is also made from potatoes, breadfruit, and manioc roots. (See BREADFRUIT; CEREALS; CORN; MANIOC; RICE; RYE; WHEAT.)

FLOWER The world would not be nearly as beautiful if there were no flowers. In our gardens we have hundreds of different kinds from all over the world. But for millions and millions of years there were no flowering plants. After flowering plants once appeared, however, they were a great success. They crowded many other plants off the earth. Most of the plants we see today have flowers.

Flowers are very important, for they produce seeds. Grass, dandelions, apple trees, and pumpkin vines would never have any seeds if they never bloomed. Neither would any other flowering plants.

Complete flowers have four parts: sepals, petals, stamens, and pistils. The pistils have in them tiny bodies called ovules. They are the beginnings of seeds. Inside ovules there are female cells called eggs. The stamens produce a fine dust called pollen. Inside the grains of pollen there are male cells called sperms.

Before ovules can become seeds they must be fertilized. Sperms from pollen grains, that is, must unite with the eggs in the ovules. What happens is this: Pollen grains in some way reach the stigma, or sticky surface, of a pistil. Tubes grow down from the pollen grains to the ovules. The sperms travel down the tubes to the eggs inside the ovules and join them.

The petals of many flowers are beautiful. They are a help in making seeds, too. As they wave in the air they attract insects. The insects find in the flowers a sweet juice called nectar. An insect crawls into a flower to get the nectar. As it does so, it brushes against the stamens and gets pollen on its body. When it goes to the next flower, some of the pollen brushes off on the pistil of that flower. This work of insects is important. For the pollen from a flower may not be able to fertilize the ovules in its own flower. A flower's perfume helps attract insects, just as its petals do.

Petals are helpful in another way. In flower buds they are wrapped around the

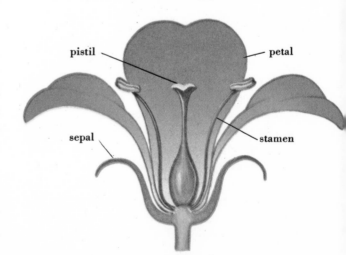

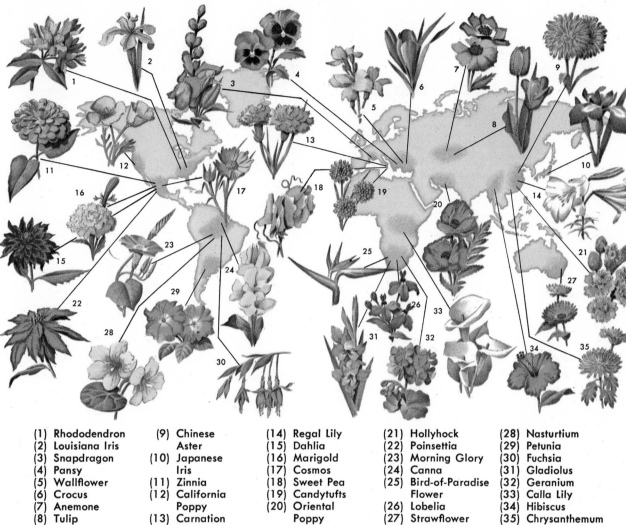

(1) Rhododendron	(9) Chinese	(14) Regal Lily	(21) Hollyhock	(28) Nasturtium
(2) Louisiana Iris	Aster	(15) Dahlia	(22) Poinsettia	(29) Petunia
(3) Snapdragon	(10) Japanese	(16) Marigold	(23) Morning Glory	(30) Fuchsia
(4) Pansy	Iris	(17) Cosmos	(24) Canna	(31) Gladiolus
(5) Wallflower	(11) Zinnia	(18) Sweet Pea	(25) Bird-of-Paradise	(32) Geranium
(6) Crocus	(12) California	(19) Candytufts	Flower	(33) Calla Lily
(7) Anemone	Poppy	(20) Oriental	(26) Lobelia	(34) Hibiscus
(8) Tulip	(13) Carnation	Poppy	(27) Strawflower	(35) Chrysanthemum

stamens and pistils and help protect them. A flower's petals may be joined together. Morning glories and petunias are examples.

The sepals of a flower may be as beautiful as the petals. They are, for instance, in the iris. But often the sepals are small and green. In buds they are on the outside and help protect the rest of the flower. Sometimes a flower's sepals are joined together to form a little cup.

A flower does not have to have all four parts. Many flowers do not have petals. Most of those without petals must depend on the wind to carry their pollen. Many flowers do not have sepals. Many do not have both stamens and pistils. Flowers must have either stamens or pistils to be of use to the plants they grow on. There are a few freak flowers that have neither. Snowball flowers are among them. There are never any snowball seeds. New snowball bushes are raised from cuttings.

Stamens, pistils, sepals, and petals may be different shapes and sizes. Each flower itself has its own special size and shape. Each one has its own special number, too. A pansy, for instance, has five sepals, five petals, five stamens, and one pistil.

Some flowers are so small that they are not usually recognized as flowers. Many people never guess that the pussies of the pussy willow and the tails of foxtail grass are bunches of flowers. But they are, and the flowers form or help to form seeds, just as larger, showier flowers do. (See POLLINATION.)

MONOCOTS

 CATTAIL FAMILY—Cattails

 WATER-PLANTAIN FAMILY—Arrow-head, Water Plantain

 GRASS FAMILY—Corn, Wheat, Rye, Oats, Bamboo, Sugarcane, Bluegrass, Broomcorn, Timothy, Foxtail Grass, Rice, Sorghum, Barley

 SEDGE FAMILY—Sedge, Bulrush, Umbrella Plant, Spike Rush, Papyrus

 PALM FAMILY—Coconut, Date, Raffia, Rattan, Royal, Palmetto

 PINEAPPLE FAMILY—Pineapple, Long Moss, Pinguin

 LILY FAMILY—Onion, Day Lily, Easter Lily, Dogtooth Violet, Star-of-Bethlehem, Hyacinth, Asparagus, Lily of the Valley, Trillium, Tulip, Tiger Lily, Garlic, Yucca, Jack-in-the-pulpit

 AMARYLLIS FAMILY—Daffodil, Poet's Narcissus, Century Plant, Amaryllis

 IRIS FAMILY—Iris, Blue-eyed Grass, Crocus, Gladiolus

 ORCHID FAMILY—Showy Lady's-slipper, Orchid, Vanilla, Moccasin Flower, Orchis, Ladies' Tresses

FLOWER FAMILIES The morning glory and sweet potato are cousins. They both belong to the morning-glory family. The tomato and deadly nightshade are cousins, too. They belong to the nightshade family. Easter lily and onion, black locust and sweet pea, and bluegrass and bamboo are other strange pairs of cousins.

It is easy to see that no one can tell by their size which plants belong in the same family. The black locust is a tree, while the sweet pea is a slender vine. Finding out whether the plants are useful does not help either. It would be hard for us to get along without tomatoes as a vegetable, but deadly nightshade is a poisonous weed. Scientists have to study the flowers of flowering plants to find out which of these plants are close relatives.

Many people raise morning glories because they have beautiful blossoms. No one raises sweet potatoes for that reason. But a sweet potato flower is really much like a morning glory. It is, however, smaller than a morning glory and is always white. The flowers of onion plants are much smaller than Easter lilies, but they are the same shape. Bluegrass flowers resemble those of bamboo, and tomato flowers those

of deadly nightshade, while black locust flowers are like sweet peas.

The flowering plants are divided into two big groups. The two groups are called the monocots and the dicots. The groups get their names from differences in their seeds. "Monocot" means "one seed leaf." "Dicot" means "two seed leaves." There are many flower families in each of these big groups. The charts show some of them.

In some flower families there are hundreds of kinds of plants. Other families are small.

The biggest flower family of all is the composite family. This family gets its name because its flowers are composed of many tiny flowers. They are really whole bouquets. The daisy and the dandelion, members of this family, are flowers that everyone knows.

Many of the flowers in the composite family are beautiful. The plants of this group are not very useful in other ways. Lettuce is one of the few composites we raise for anything except their flowers.

Far more useful is the grass family. The plants in this family have such tiny flowers that most people do not think of them as flowers at all. But all our common grains are grasses. If we had to do without the grass family, we would have no wheat, rye, oats, rice, or barley. Even corn, with its big ears and big leaves, belongs to this family. So do sugarcane and all the grasses we raise in our lawns and pastures.

The rose family is another very large and important family. Of course, all the many kinds of roses belong to the family. Many pretty shrubs such as spiraea and ninebark are in the family, too. Besides, the rose family has in it a great many of our common fruits. Plums, apples, peaches, pears, apricots, cherries, blackberries, raspberries, and strawberries are all cousins of the wild rose. (See CEREALS; FLOWER; GARDEN FLOWERS; GRASSES; LEGUMES; ROSES; WILD FLOWERS.)

DICOTS

  WILLOW FAMILY—Willow, Poplar, Cottonwood, Aspen

BEECH FAMILY—Beech, Chestnut, Oak

ELM FAMILY—Elm, Hackberry

 GOOSEFOOT FAMILY—Goosefoot, Beet, Spinach, Lamb's-quarters, Russian Thistle, Chard, Good-King-Henry, Saltbush

 PINK FAMILY — Pink, Carnation, Catchfly, Bouncing Bet, Chickweed, Baby's Breath, Sweet William

 WATER-LILY FAMILY—Water Lily, Lotus, Nelumbo, Spatterdock

 BUTTERCUP FAMILY — Buttercup, Meadow Rue, Hepatica, Anemone, Monkshood, Marsh Marigold, Columbine, Larkspur, Peony, Clematis

 POPPY FAMILY—Poppy, Bloodroot, Prickly Poppy, California Poppy

 MUSTARD FAMILY—Mustard, Sweet Alyssum, Peppergrass, Radish, Turnip, Cabbage, Watercress, Cauliflower, Shepherd's Purse, Candytuft

 ROSE FAMILY—Rose, Spiraea, Hawthorn, Strawberry, Plum, Apple, Peach, Pear, Cherry, Blackberry, Raspberry, Mountain Ash

  PEA FAMILY—Pea, Sweet Pea, Bean, Alfalfa, Clover, Lupine, Peanut, Locust, Honey Locust, Vetch, Kentucky Coffee Tree, Redbud, Licorice

 VIOLET FAMILY—Violet, Pansy, Viola

 PARSLEY FAMILY—Parsley, Carrot, Parsnip, Celery, Queen Anne's Lace, Caraway, Dill, Poison Hemlock

 HEATH FAMILY — Heather, Wintergreen, Leatherleaf, Rhododendron, Kinnikinick, Huckleberry, Blueberry, Cranberry, Trailing Arbutus, Azalea, Mountain Laurel

 PRIMROSE FAMILY—Primrose, Pimpernel, Loosestrife, Cyclamen, Starflower, Shooting Star, Cowslip

 MILKWEED FAMILY—Milkweed, Butterfly Weed, Anglepod

 MORNING-GLORY FAMILY—Morning Glory, Bindweed, Dodder, Sweet Potato, Moonflower

 MINT FAMILY—Peppermint, Spearmint, Catnip, Sage, Horsemint, Thyme, Horehound, Marjoram, Salvia, Skullcap, Selfheal, Lavender

 NIGHTSHADE FAMILY—Nightshade, Eggplant, Potato, Petunia, Tomato, Tobacco, Groundcherry, Matrimony Vine, Green Pepper

 HONEYSUCKLE FAMILY—Honeysuckle, Twinflower, Snowberry, Highbush Cranberry, Elder, Snowball

 GOURD FAMILY—Gourd, Pumpkin, Squash, Cucumber, Watermelon

 COMPOSITE FAMILY—Daisy, Sunflower, Aster, Goldenrod, Ragweed, Bachelor's Button, Dandelion, Marigold, Cosmos, Zinnia, Scotch Thistle, Lettuce, Coneflower, Artichoke

FOG A fog is a cloud close to the ground. Clouds are made of tiny drops of water or crystals of ice. So are fogs. There may be so many of these droplets or crystals that they shut off the view of everything round about. There are many accidents in fogs because people cannot see their way. Airplane pilots and travelers on highways are warned by radio of dense fogs.

Most fogs are made of water droplets. Such fogs are common near big bodies of water. The land is likely to cool off much faster than the water. Warm, moist air moving in over the land is cooled quickly. Some of the water vapor in the air changes to droplets of water and forms a fog. In cities fog may have so much smoke mixed with it that it is called smog.

Some cities are famous for their fogs and smogs. London is one of them.

Fogs disappear when the ground warms up or when a brisk wind blows them away. They can be driven away by fires. During World War II millions of dollars were spent clearing airfields of fog. Fogs at airports are still a problem. Now, however, by using radio, radar, and powerful lights, planes can be guided to make safe landings and take-offs in all but the thickest of fogs.

FOLK SONGS Before the days of machines people often sang as they worked. Men sang as they swung their scythes in a field of wheat, felled a tree in a forest, or rowed a boat down a river. Women sang as they churned butter or spun wool into yarn. Children still sometimes play singing games. Grown-ups almost never do, but they once did. Songs that have grown naturally from the work and play of people are called folk songs. Such songs have been handed down from generation to generation. Each generation may change a song somewhat.

Today folk songs are very popular. Usually they are sung to the accompaniment of a guitar or some other simple instrument. There are musicians, however, who think that folk songs should be sung without any accompaniment.

Many folk songs tell the stories of people and of events. They all tell much about the people who first sang them. Folk songs, a famous writer has said, are the musical mirror of the world.

FOODS Pickled ants, smoked seaworms, blubber, fried tadpoles—to some people these are fine foods. Many of our foods would be just as strange to people of other lands. But whether we eat pickled ants or pickled peaches, smoked seaworms or smoked ham, blubber or butter, food serves the same purpose for us all.

In the first place food is a fuel. It keeps our bodies running. It gives us energy to work and play. It keeps us warm, too. It does for us very much the same things gasoline does for an automobile.

But it does much more for us than gasoline does for an automobile. No one expects his automobile to get bigger because he keeps putting gasoline in it. He does not expect the gasoline to mend a punctured tire, either. But our food makes us grow, and it furnishes the materials we have to have to mend cut fingers and broken bones. Food also gives us materials that make our bodies run in just the right way.

Getting the food we need does not mean the same thing as getting enough food. Sugar, for instance, is good food. It gives us a great deal of energy. But we could not live on pure sugar. It does not have any building materials in it. It makes us go but not grow. We need food for so many different kinds of things that we have to have many different kinds of foods. Milk is sometimes called a perfect food. Actually it is a perfect food only for little babies. But it is one of the foods all growing boys and girls should have.

Some of the foods we eat are especially good for us because they have vitamins in them. Vitamins are marvelous substances that help keep our bodies working as they should. We get many of the vitamins we need from fruits and vegetables.

Some of the foods we eat are especially good for us because they have in them minerals we need. Some minerals are necessary for building strong bones and strong teeth. Cereals are one of the kinds of foods that furnish the minerals we need.

Meat and eggs are good for building muscles. They are good "grow" foods.

A person should know what foods he needs and how much he should eat of each. The chart here is a simple guide. A day's vegetables and fruits should include one rich in vitamin C and one rich in vitamin A. (See CALORIE; MINERALS; VITAMINS.)

Vegetable-Fruit Group
(Four Servings a Day)

Milk Group
(A Quart a Day)

Meat Group
(Two Servings a Day)

Bread-Cereal Group
(Four Servings a Day)

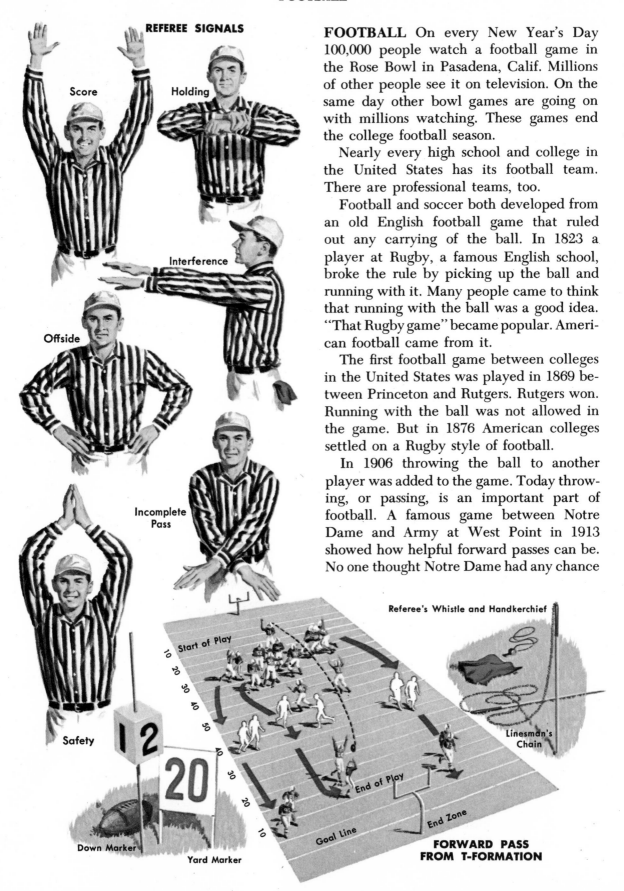

REFEREE SIGNALS

Score

Holding

Interference

Offside

Incomplete Pass

Safety

Down Marker

Yard Marker

Referee's Whistle and Handkerchief

Linesman's Chain

Start of Play

End of Play

Goal Line

End Zone

FORWARD PASS FROM T-FORMATION

FOOTBALL On every New Year's Day 100,000 people watch a football game in the Rose Bowl in Pasadena, Calif. Millions of other people see it on television. On the same day other bowl games are going on with millions watching. These games end the college football season.

Nearly every high school and college in the United States has its football team. There are professional teams, too.

Football and soccer both developed from an old English football game that ruled out any carrying of the ball. In 1823 a player at Rugby, a famous English school, broke the rule by picking up the ball and running with it. Many people came to think that running with the ball was a good idea. "That Rugby game" became popular. American football came from it.

The first football game between colleges in the United States was played in 1869 between Princeton and Rutgers. Rutgers won. Running with the ball was not allowed in the game. But in 1876 American colleges settled on a Rugby style of football.

In 1906 throwing the ball to another player was added to the game. Today throwing, or passing, is an important part of football. A famous game between Notre Dame and Army at West Point in 1913 showed how helpful forward passes can be. No one thought Notre Dame had any chance at all of winning. But Notre Dame won 35 to 13 by its passing.

A football game is played in two 30-minute halves, each divided into two 15-minute quarters. Eleven men make up a team—7 linemen and 4 in the backfield. The playing field, or gridiron, is 300 feet long and 160 feet wide. At its ends are the goal lines and goalposts.

Each team tries to get the ball over the other team's goal line. The team that has the ball has four chances, or downs, to move the ball forward 10 yards. If it succeeds, it has four more downs to move the ball forward another 10 yards. If it fails, the other team gets the ball.

Scores are made in five ways: Carrying or passing the ball over the goal line is a touchdown. It counts 6 points. Kicking the ball over the crossbar between the goalposts after a touchdown adds 1 point. Getting the ball across the goal line in some other way after a touchdown adds 2 points. A field goal—kicking a goal without first making a touchdown—counts 3 points. If a player with the ball is downed behind his own goal line, the other side gets 2 points for a safety.

Football is rough. To keep it from being too rough and to see that its many complicated rules are followed, there must be several officials for each game.

Football teams have coaches who help them work out plays. A good coach means a great deal to a team. There have been many famous coaches, among them Glenn ("Pop") Warner, Amos Alonzo Stagg, and Knute Rockne. At the Carlisle Indian school Warner developed the Indian athlete Jim Thorpe into an all-American star. Stagg coached for many years at the University of Chicago, then at the College of the Pacific. He earned the name of "grand old man." Rockne was the coach of Notre Dame teams that won 105 games, tied in 5, and lost only 12. His great 1924 team was famous for "the Four Horsemen" that made up its backfield. (See SOCCER.)

FORAGE CROPS Any crop is a forage crop if practically the whole plant is good food for farm animals. The most important forage crops are certain grasses. Among them are timothy, bluegrass, and fescue. Some of the legumes are also important forage crops. Clover and alfalfa are two. Alfalfa has been raised longer than any other forage crop. Many grasses and legumes are good grazing crops—animals, that is, walk over the pasture where the plants are growing and nip off the tops of the plants. These grazing crops can also be made into hay as winter food for stock. They can, that is, be cut and dried. Some forage crops are better as hay than as green pasture. Alfalfa is one.

Corn, although raised in most regions chiefly for its grain, may also be called a forage crop. While it is green the stems, leaves, and young ears are sometimes cut into small pieces and stored in silos. The cut-up corn, or silage, stays green and makes excellent food for cattle in the wintertime. Sorghums and millets, like corn, may be raised for their grain, or the whole plants may be used as hay or silage. (See CORN; GRASSES; LEGUMES.)

FORD, HENRY (1863–1947) The United States is a great industrial nation. Many Americans have made huge fortunes in industry. Henry Ford built up one of the largest fortunes ever made in this country. He made it by manufacturing automobiles.

Henry Ford was born on a farm near Dearborn, Mich. Even as a young boy he was much interested in machinery. Instead of playing outdoors he would sit at a workbench and mend clocks and watches for the neighbors. The tools he used in repairing the first watch he worked on were a shingle nail, some knitting needles, and a pair of tweezers made out of a corset stay.

Henry Ford's mother died when he was 12. Four years later he left the farm to work in a machine shop. When he was 21, his father gave him 40 acres of land, hoping that he would give up his work with machines. Ford tried farming, but his interest in machines was too great. He went to work for the Detroit Edison Company.

Ford was now much interested in horseless carriages. He decided to build one himself. Night after night he worked on it. At last, at two o'clock one rainy night in May, 1896, the car was ready for a trial run. Ford trundled it out and ran it around the block. It worked well.

Ford later sold his first car for $200 and built a better one. Soon the sight of Ford riding about in his automobile was a common one. The mayor of Detroit gave him the first driver's license ever issued.

Other cars were being manufactured, but they were all expensive. Ford wanted to build a car that was cheap enough for most families to own. It was hard for him to find anyone willing to put money into the company he had in mind. But by building two racing cars he succeeded in getting people interested in his company. One of the racing cars was the "999." It won every race it entered. At last, in 1903, the Ford Motor Company was formed.

Ford's regular cars soon were popular. They were very dependable. Roads too

Model T, 1914

1903

rough and muddy for other cars did not stop them. Ford's famous Model T was said to be "as frisky as a jackrabbit and more durable than a mule." In the beginning doctors and farmers were the best customers. But others followed.

Money came pouring in. As Fords were made by the hundreds, by the thousands, and then by the millions, money came in by the hundreds and the thousands and the millions of dollars. Ford made a fortune for many others besides himself. One woman who put only $100 in the Ford Motor Company in the beginning sold her share later for $260,000.

Ford could make good cheap cars partly because he had in his factory an assembly line. The cars being built were moved slowly past one worker after another. Each worker had just one tool and did just one bit of work. The cars rolled off the assembly line ready to be sold.

Many famous men were friends of Ford. Among them were Thomas Edison, John Burroughs, and Harvey Firestone. Among them also were several presidents.

Some of his great fortune Ford spent in interesting ways. Near his old Dearborn home he built Greenfield Village. In it there are reproductions of many buildings famous in American history. In Massachusetts he rebuilt the Wayside Inn, which Longfellow made famous. During World War I he chartered a ship and went to Europe on a peace crusade to end the war. (See AUTOMOBILES; INDUSTRIES.)

FORESTS AND FORESTRY Trees are our biggest plants. Great groups of these giant plants are called forests. There have been forests on the earth for at least 350 million years, but the first forests did not look much like those of today. The trees in them were not oaks, pines, or maples. Instead they were club mosses and horsetails.

In some forests of today the trees are all the same kind. A forest may be, for instance, a pure stand of Douglas fir. But in most forests there are several kinds of trees.

FOREST PRODUCTS

The thickest forests are in the hot, wet lands of the tropics. The many trees have to fight for sunlight. There is plenty of warmth and moisture, but to get enough sunlight a tree may have to grow tall enough to reach up above its neighbors.

The forests of a country are a part of its riches. Forests, of course, furnish lumber for building and wood for such things as paper and plastics. Some forest trees furnish nuts or fruits or maple sugar. Others furnish such things as drugs and turpentine. The diagram on the page before this gives some idea of the great variety of products we owe to forests.

Even without their products forests would be valuable. They slow down the runoff of rainwater into streams and help to prevent floods. They furnish homes for many smaller plants and for many animals.

What plants and animals a forest holds depends chiefly on where the forest is. No one would expect to find the same dwellers in a tropical rain forest that one finds in, let us say, a forest on northern mountain slopes. But any forest is much like a city made up of buildings crowded close together. Different living things live at different levels. In the trees themselves there are such animals as woodpeckers, owls, squirrels, opossums, porcupines, tree frogs, and monkeys. Vines climb up the trees. Air plants perch on the branches, and shelf fungi and lichens grow on the trunks. In the bushes under the trees little birds such as warblers nest. Chipmunks, foxes, shrews, ovenbirds, wood frogs, ferns, and mushrooms live on the forest floor. In the soil itself there are moles, worms, and vast numbers of bacteria. And at every level of a forest there are innumerable insects.

In the early days of the United States much of the land, as the little map shows, was forested. Some forests were conifer forests, made up of such trees as pines, firs, hemlocks, and spruces. The Pacific coast and Rocky Mountain forests are in this group. Others were hardwood forests,

made up mostly of such trees as oaks, maples, and hickories. The forests of the central eastern region belong here. Still others had in them a mixture of hardwoods and conifers. Both the northeastern and the southern forests are in this group.

The first settlers had to cut down trees to get land for farming. There were so many trees that no one thought of being careful of them. But the country grew fast. And the forests disappeared fast. When the Pilgrims came to America in 1620 the region that became the United States had about 1,030,000,000 acres of forest. Three hundred years later there were only 608,000,000 acres and much of that was no longer virgin forest—forest from which no trees had been cut. At last Americans realized that their forests might soon be gone. They began to plan ways of saving those left and replanting empty areas that had been stripped of their trees.

People did not cut down all the forests that have disappeared. Fires have destroyed many forests. Some of these fires were caused by lightning. Others have been traced back to campfires that were not put out or to lighted cigarettes that were tossed carelessly away. Tree diseases and insects are great enemies of our forests, too.

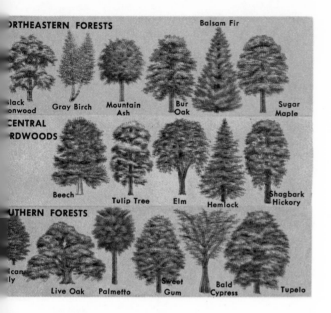

NORTHEASTERN FORESTS

Black Cottonwood · Gray Birch · Mountain Ash · Bur Oak · Balsam Fir · Sugar Maple

CENTRAL HARDWOODS

Beech · Tulip Tree · Elm · Hemlock · Shagbark Hickory

SOUTHERN FORESTS

American Holly · Live Oak · Palmetto · Sweet Gum · Bald Cypress · Tupelo

The United States government now owns a great deal of the forest land left in the country. For the most part the national forests are carefully supervised by men trained to look after the cutting and care of trees.

In the national forests there are also forest rangers. From high lookout towers they watch for fires. If one is sighted, a crew of fire fighters goes to fight it.

The rangers watch for signs of disease and insect pests, too. Often trees with a disease are cut down and hauled out of the forest so that the disease will not spread to healthy trees. Forests may also be sprayed from airplanes in fighting diseases and insects. The spray used is not always an insecticide. A virus, for example, has been found very useful in combating a kind of sawfly that attacks pine trees. Worldwide searches are made for natural enemies of insect pests.

Private companies that own forest lands are taking good care of them, too. They are cutting trees from them carefully. They have nurseries for raising young trees, and they are experimenting with hybrids. They hope to get varieties that will grow faster, taller, and bigger around, and be better able to hold their own against insects and diseases than those we have now. Growers want to be able to harvest crops of lumber for years to come.

Better care of the forests has paid off. The amount of forest has gone up to about 775,000,000 acres. More important still, the amount of new wood is now keeping up with the amount cut each year.

Even if no one ever cut down a forest tree and even if trees had no enemies, forests would not always stay the same. Some kinds of trees are pioneers. They prepare the way for other trees. On some of the sand dunes of Lake Michigan, for instance, jack pines grow. After there is a thick stand of jack pines the forest is too shady for little pines. But it is right for maples and beeches. The jack pines gradually give way to maples and beeches.

Knowing that some trees must have the way paved for them helps us understand why a forest fire may do more damage than just the burning down of thousands of trees. In many cases the forest cannot simply be replanted. A very long time may be needed to get the region ready again for the trees that once grew there. Perhaps visitors to forests would be more careful if they knew that a campfire or a burning cigarette may do damage that cannot be undone for centuries. (See CONIFERS; CONSERVATION; FIRE FIGHTING; JUNGLE; LUMBERING; PAPER; TREES; WOOD.)

Original Forest Land in the United States

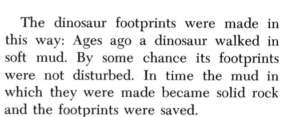

Sabertooth

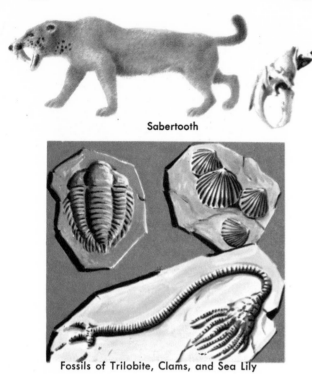

Fossils of Trilobite, Clams, and Sea Lily

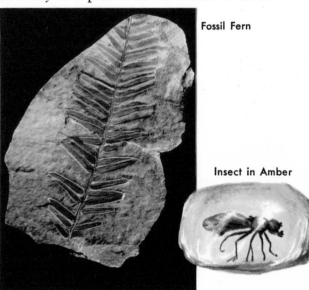

Sabertooth Skeleton

FOSSILS Many plants and animals that once lived on the earth have disappeared. There were once dinosaurs far bigger than elephants. There were once horsetail plants that grew to be big trees. For millions of years the seashores swarmed with trilobites. During the time called the great Ice Age there were sabertooths with teeth like knives, and rhinoceroses with long, shaggy hair. We know about these ancient living things and many others because we have fossils of them. Fossils are traces found in rocks of the living things of long ago.

A fossil may be a whole animal that was buried in such a way that the body did not decay. Many mammoths have been found in the Far North frozen in great blocks of ice left from the Ice Age.

The sticky gum of ancient pine trees trapped and preserved whole insects. Later the gum hardened into amber.

The sabertooth skeleton pictured is made up of bones kept from decaying by the tar, or asphalt, of the famous tar pools in California. Thousands of animals trapped in the sticky tar of those pools sank beneath the surface and were buried there.

The dinosaur footprints were made in this way: Ages ago a dinosaur walked in soft mud. By some chance its footprints were not disturbed. In time the mud in which they were made became solid rock and the footprints were saved.

The bones of the fossil fish pictured are petrified. Many fossil bones are petrified. "Petrified" means "changed to stone." Often a backboned animal died, sank to the bottom of some body of water, and was covered with sand or mud. Soon nothing was left but its bones. Then little by little the water brought minerals and filled up every tiny space in the bone. The minerals shut the air away and preserved the bone. In some

Fossil Fern

Insect in Amber

cases all the bone itself was taken away, tiny particle by tiny particle, and replaced with minerals.

In petrified wood there is no wood left. As the trunks of ancient trees that died lay covered with mud, water carrying minerals rebuilt them in solid stone.

Several of the fossils pictured are casts. As the caption tells you, the trilobite fossil shown on this page is one. It was made in

Trilobite and Lamp Shell

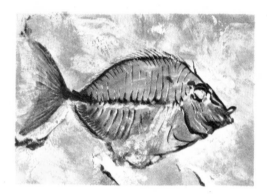

Fish Fossil

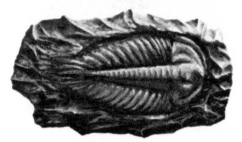

Cast of Trilobite

very much the same way we make plaster casts. A trilobite of long ago died in the shallow water near the shore of the sea. It was covered with sand and mud. Its body decayed, but it left a space where it had been. The walls of this space acted as a mold. Limy mud filled up the mold. In time this limy mud hardened into solid stone. Many leaf fossils are casts.

Most fossils are found in rocks formed underwater. Sandstone, limestone, and shale are common water-made rocks.

In today's museums there are millions of fossils, collected by scientists from all over the world. Fossils tell a wonderful story of living things of long, long ago. (See AMBER; DINOSAURS; EARTH HISTORY; PETRIFIED WOOD; TRILOBITE.)

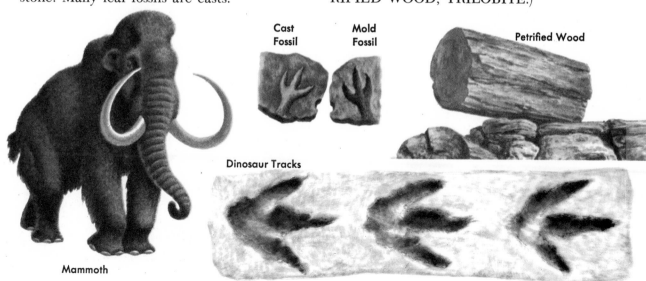

Cast Fossil

Mold Fossil

Petrified Wood

Dinosaur Tracks

Mammoth

FOSTER, STEPHEN C. (1826-1864) "My Old Kentucky Home," "Oh! Susanna," and "Old Folks at Home" are songs that almost everyone in the United States knows. They are among the more than 200 songs written by Stephen Foster. Many of his songs were sung by the original Christy's minstrels and other Negro minstrel troupes.

Foster wrote a song almost as easily as most of us write letters. But he did not lead a very happy life. Thousands and thousands of copies of his songs were sold, but he did not make much money from them. He died homeless, almost friendless, and without any money. He was only 38 years old. Probably he did not guess that his songs would live long after he died.

There are several memorials to Stephen Foster. One is in Pittsburgh, where Foster was born. Another is at White Springs, Fla., on the Suwannee River, made famous by "Old Folks at Home."

"My Old Kentucky Home" is certain to be heard from coast to coast at least once every year. Now the state song of Kentucky, this song is played each year just before the famous Kentucky Derby is run.

FOUNTAIN One of the most photographed fountains in the world is the fountain of Prometheus at Rockefeller Center, New York. Many ribbons of water come from the sides of the fountain toward the center. Lights underneath the water make the whole fountain glow. Every year hundreds of thousands of visitors from far and wide see this famous fountain.

For centuries people have enjoyed watching fountains play. There were fountains in old Greek and Roman gardens. Fountains are common today.

The Buckingham Memorial Fountain in Chicago is another beautiful American fountain. Big crowds gather on summer evenings to watch its many sprays of water shoot high into the air as changing colored lights play on them. The Cranbrook fountain in a suburb of Detroit is one of the many fountains made by the famous Swedish sculptor Carl Milles. Many other American cities can boast of beautiful fountains.

To see the Neptune Fountain, one would have to visit the gardens of Versailles near Paris. The gardens are on the grounds of a royal palace where kings of France once

Rockefeller Center

Neptune, Versailles

Trevi, Rome

Cranbrook

Buckingham, Chicago

FOURTH OF JULY Another name for the Fourth of July is Independence Day. The day is a holiday set aside in the United States to celebrate the adopting of the Declaration of Independence.

The Continental Congress adopted the Declaration of Independence on July 4, 1776. In 1783 the state of Pennsylvania made July 4 a legal holiday. Other states followed Pennsylvania's lead. Now it is our greatest patriotic holiday.

All the cities and many of the towns of America have big celebrations on the Fourth of July. Flags fly from public buildings, and from many other buildings, too. There are big parades, picnics, ball games, and displays of fireworks. Children used to celebrate with firecrackers and fireworks and cap pistols. But many were hurt. Now it is against the law in many states to sell fireworks, firecrackers, and caps for pistols. Big public fireworks displays managed by well-trained workers have taken the place of small displays in people's backyards.

Very fittingly, on July 4, 1850, the cornerstone of the Washington Monument was laid. (See DECLARATION OF INDEPENDENCE; HOLIDAYS.)

lived. The charming spouting goose is in a park in Copenhagen. A motion picture, *Three Coins in a Fountain*, made the Trevi Fountain in Rome even more famous than it had been before.

An artesian well—one that flows by itself —may spout high enough to form a natural fountain. Here the weight of the water in a sloping layer of rock deep underground forces the water out. In artificial fountains it may be forced out by the weight of the water in a reservoir. But in most cases it is forced out with pumps. The Prometheus fountain has three pumps. Two work at a time. They pump 4,000 gallons of water a minute. The water flows from the pool of the fountain to big tanks and is pumped over and over again.

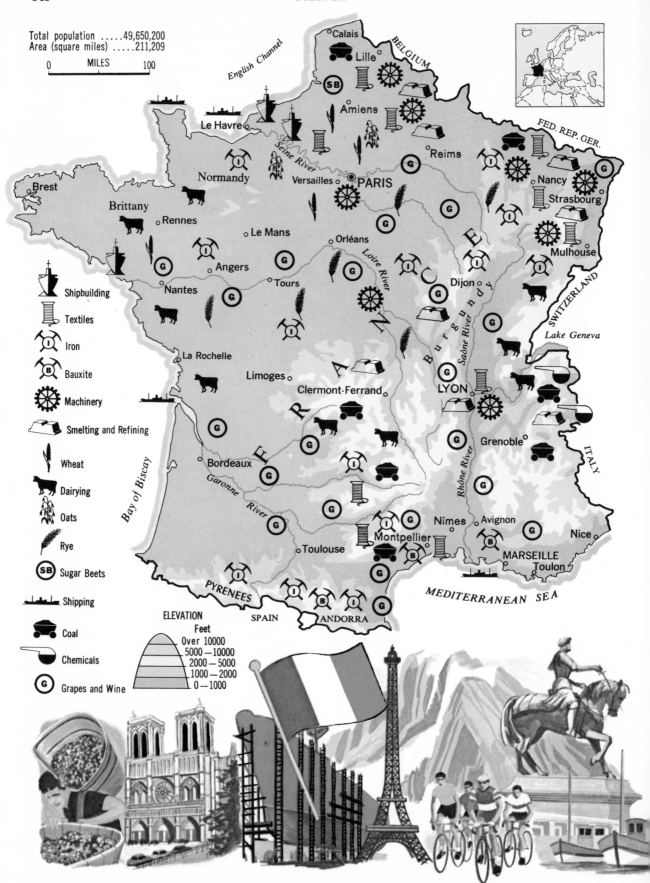

Total population 49,650,200
Area (square miles) 211,209

0   MILES   100

Legend

Shipbuilding
Textiles
Iron
Bauxite
Machinery
Smelting and Refining
Wheat
Dairying
Oats
Rye
SB Sugar Beets
Shipping
Coal
Chemicals
G Grapes and Wine

ELEVATION
Feet
Over 10000
5000 — 10000
2000 — 5000
1000 — 2000
0 — 1000

Places and features

English Channel
Calais
Lille
BELGIUM
Le Havre
Amiens
Reims
FED. REP. GER.
Seine River
Normandy
Versailles
PARIS
Nancy
Strasbourg
Brest
Brittany
Rennes
Le Mans
Orléans
Mulhouse
Angers
Nantes
Tours
Loire River
Dijon
SWITZERLAND
Lake Geneva
La Rochelle
Limoges
Clermont-Ferrand
Burgundy
Saône River
LYON
Grenoble
ITALY
Bay of Biscay
Bordeaux
Garonne River
Rhône River
Toulouse
Montpellier
Nîmes
Avignon
Nice
PYRENEES
SPAIN
ANDORRA
MARSEILLE
Toulon
MEDITERRANEAN SEA
FRANCE

FRANCE Although it is not as big as the state of Texas, France is the second largest of the many countries of Europe. The only country that spreads over more of Europe is the huge Soviet Union.

Paris, France's famous capital, is about 140 miles farther north than Quebec, Canada. Even Marseilles on France's southern coast is as far north as Portland, Me. But all over France winters are mild. Much lowland borders the north and west coasts and the many rivers.

About a fifth of France's workers are farmers. Many visitors go to see the gardens and orchards near Paris, and the farms in Brittany to the west. Near those farms there are quaint fishing villages. The farmers raise oats, potatoes, and apples.

Near Marseilles there are vineyards, almond groves, rice fields, and fields of flowers raised for perfumes. The region of the Garonne River in southwestern France is a "land of corn and wine." Farther north much wheat and barley are raised. On the plateau in southern France farmers keep sheep and goats. Roquefort cheese is made there. Throughout France more and more farmers are raising cattle.

The cities of France are as varied as its farms. Lyons is famous as a silk-weaving city, Bordeaux as a wine port, and Nice as a resort. Near rich iron mines in northeastern France there are many steel mills. And perfumes and chemicals rank high among French factory products. Many millions of people in France depend on factory work or trade for their living.

France has thousands of miles of water highways. Besides the rivers, there are many canals. Roads, railroads, and airways also crisscross the country.

Many things in France today are reminders of its very long past. In ancient times it was called Gaul. The Romans conquered Gaul 2,000 years ago. Still to be seen there are ruins of some of the wonderful roads and aqueducts they built. The Romans spread their learning in Gaul. Most French words come from Latin, the language of the Romans. Christianity spread through Gaul during Roman times, too.

Gaul had been a Roman province for 500 years when it was conquered by tribes from the north. They were the Franks. The name "France" comes from their name. The Franks learned much from the people they ruled. The greatest Frankish ruler was Charlemagne, who became king in 768.

Between 900 and 700 years ago, French kings and nobles took part in Crusades to the Holy Land. Many of France's great cathedrals were built during that time. Trade began to increase, and towns grew.

One of the most important French holidays, the second Sunday in May, is in honor of Joan of Arc. She helped to bring victory to France to end the Hundred Years' War with England. It ended in 1453, less than 40 years before America was discovered.

Not long after the American Revolution, the French Revolution made France a republic. But soon Napoleon made himself emperor. Then he was overthrown. For more than 50 years after Napoleon, France was ruled by kings again. But since 1871 it has been once more a republic.

French explorers played an important part in opening up the New World. Eastern Canada was settled by the French more than 300 years ago. Later the region was taken over by the English. The United States bought from France the vast stretch of land known as the Louisiana Purchase.

In the scramble for Africa in the late 1800's France established many colonies there. Since World War II most of them have become independent. In the main, however, they continue to have strong ties with France as members of the French Community. France still has some other lands overseas. Among them are French Guiana in South America and numerous islands in the Atlantic, Pacific, and Indian Oceans. (See CHARLEMAGNE; JOAN OF ARC; NAPOLEON; PARIS; ROLAND; WORLD WAR I; WORLD WAR II.)

FRANKLIN, BENJAMIN (1706–1790) Any list of great American statesmen is sure to have the name of Benjamin Franklin. He did a great deal to win friends for the United States in its earliest days. But Franklin would be a famous American even if he had not been a great statesman. He was also a great patriot, writer, and publisher. He invented many useful things. And he made important scientific discoveries.

Franklin was born in Boston. He was the 15th child in the family. When he was only 10, Benjamin went to work in his father's candle- and soapmaking shop. Two years later he went to work in his brother's printshop. The two brothers did not get on well together. At 17 Benjamin ran away to Philadelphia to find work.

With a loaf of bread under one arm and only a few cents in his pocket, he looked for a printshop that would hire him. He found one. Six years later he owned his own printshop. In it he started a newspaper—the *Pennsylvania Gazette*—and a magazine—the *General Magazine*. He also published *Poor Richard's Almanack*, which he wrote himself. The almanac had many wise sayings in it. One such saying is:

Early to bed, early to rise,

Makes a man healthy, wealthy, and wise.

Franklin's printshop did not take all his time. He carried on many science experiments and worked on various inventions.

The picture shows his most famous experiment. By flying a kite in a thunderstorm, he discovered that lightning is a huge spark of electricity. Among his inventions are bifocals and the Franklin stove. He also found time to serve the colony of Pennsylvania in many ways. For years he was a postmaster general for all the colonies.

After he was 50 Franklin spent many years in Europe representing the colonies. At first he was in England. But when he found that the colonies wanted their freedom, he returned to America. He helped write the Declaration of Independence and was one of the patriots who signed it. He then went to France. There he won help for the colonies in their war with England.

After the war was over, Franklin again returned to America. He was nearly 80, but the young country needed his help. He was called on to work on the Constitution.

Franklin guessed that his life would be interesting to others. He wrote a wonderful account of it in his *Autobiography*. (See DECLARATION OF INDEPENDENCE; LIGHTNING; U.S. POSTAL SERVICE.)

Franklin's Most Famous Experiment

FRECKLES Every person who is not an albino has some coloring matter in his skin. This coloring matter is called pigment. Some races have more pigment in their skins than other races. Negroes and Indians, for instance, have a great deal.

When a light-skinned person stays out of doors in the sun for hours at a time, he usually gets tanned. He gets tanned because the sunshine makes more pigment form in his skin. Sometimes the pigment comes in spots instead of in an allover coat of tan. These spots we call freckles.

Freckles and red hair seem to go together. Perhaps red-haired people are more likely to have freckles than other people because they are nearly always fair.

FREUD, SIGMUND (1856–1939) Psychiatry is a branch of medicine. It has to do with mental health. Sigmund Freud is one of the great names in this field. He became famous for founding psychoanalysis, a way of treating patients who are mentally or emotionally disturbed.

Freud was born in Austria. In 1938, after nearly 80 years in Vienna, he went to England to get away from the Nazis. He died there shortly afterward.

FRICTION It is hard to push a piece of sandpaper over a rough piece of wood. There is, we say, a great deal of friction between the sandpaper and the wood. It is hard to pull a big box loaded with rocks along a concrete sidewalk. There is a great deal of friction between the box and the sidewalk. Whenever two surfaces rub together there is some friction. But the friction is greater if the surfaces are rough than if they are smooth.

Friction produces heat. An eraser used to rub out a pencil mark gets warm. Sometimes there is a hotbox in the wheel of a train because there has been too much friction between the wheel and the axle. Scratching a kitchen match on sandpaper makes the match so hot that it lights.

Putting oil or grease between the two surfaces that are rubbing together is one way of making friction less. Using rollers or wheels or ball bearings is another.

Friction makes our coats wear out at the elbows. It makes us have to buy new automobile tires and new shoes. It costs us a great deal for oil and grease and wheels and ball bearings.

But it is a good thing that there is some friction. Without it no knot would stay tied. Nails driven into wood would not hold. We could not go anywhere in a train or an automobile. The wheels would spin round and round in the same place. We could not even walk about. Floors and sidewalks would be far slicker than ice. For astronauts taking walks out in space the lack of friction there is a problem.

Frost on Windowpanes

FROST Frost may be like a fairy forest on a windowpane in the winter. Frost is ice. It is formed when moist air comes against something very cold. The water vapor in the air freezes.

Frost on windowpanes is on the inside of the windows. The moisture comes from the warm air inside the building. The glass is cooled by the cold air outside. The frost on windows is like the frost that forms on refrigerator coils and in freezers, but it is in pretty patterns.

At night in spring and fall frost often forms on grass and roofs and bushes and on cars parked out of doors. Of course, it does not form unless the temperature goes below freezing. Above freezing, dew forms instead. (See DEW.)

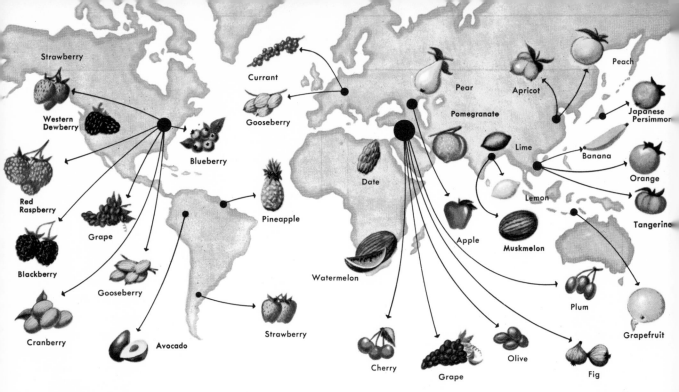

Strawberry · Currant · Pear · Apricot · Peach · Western Dewberry · Gooseberry · Pomegranate · Japanese Persimmon · Blueberry · Lime · Banana · Red Raspberry · Date · Lemon · Orange · Grape · Pineapple · Apple · Muskmelon · Tangerine · Blackberry · Gooseberry · Watermelon · Plum · Cranberry · Avocado · Strawberry · Cherry · Grape · Olive · Fig · Grapefruit

FRUITS A fruit market is an exciting place. The fruits come from many different parts of the world. There may be bananas from Central America, figs from Italy, and dates from Iraq. There may be apples from Oregon, peaches from Georgia, pineapples from Hawaii, and grapes from New York. All the year round there are oranges from Florida, Arizona, California, or Texas.

The map above was not made to show where fruits are raised now. It shows instead where the wild ancestors of our fruits lived. The map tells us, for instance, that we have Asia to thank for the peach, Europe for the currant, Africa for the watermelon, and the eastern Mediterranean region for the date and the fig. Today most people think of Hawaii when they think of pineapples, but the pineapple came originally from South America. The countries of Central America raise so many bananas that they are sometimes called the banana republics, but the banana is a native of southeastern Asia. If American fruit markets had only the fruits whose ancestors once grew wild in America, many of our best-liked fruits would be missing.

In other parts of the world, especially in the tropics, there are delicious fruits that are seldom if ever seen in our markets. Among them are the akee, the custard apple, and the mangosteen.

It is good that fruits are easy to buy, for scientists tell us that we should have some fruit every day. The chief food material in most fruits is sugar. The sugar gives them their sweet taste. Sugar is excellent for energy, and it is much better for us to get it in fruit than in the form of pure sugar. For in fruit we get vitamins and minerals along with it.

The idea of eating fruit is not new. Our cavemen ancestors probably depended a great deal on wild fruit. But how surprised a caveman would be in one of our fruit stores! We have more kinds of fruit than our early ancestors ever dreamed of. And our fruits are bigger and more beautiful than any the cavemen found growing wild.

The pictures show many of our fruits of today. There are others besides.

Fruits are seed packages. The seeds in such packages have a good chance of getting scattered since they are in fruits that are good to eat. Birds and other animals may carry the fruits away, eat the pulpy part, and drop the seeds. The seeds may fall in good places for growing.

Some fruits have only one seed. Peaches, plums, cherries, and apricots are good examples. Some have several seeds. Grapes, apples, oranges, and pears do. Some, like watermelons, cantaloupes, strawberries, and blackberries, have many seeds.

Fruits come from flowers. Before a pear orchard, for instance, can have any pears on its trees, the trees must bloom. If a late frost kills the blossoms, there will be no pear crop.

Most of the fruit trees in our orchards are grafted trees. Grafted trees come into bearing sooner than trees raised from seeds. Besides, the orchard owner is much surer with grafted trees of getting exactly the variety of fruit he wants. The apples on a tree raised from seed may be quite different from the apple the seed came from.

But fruit trees sometimes are raised from seeds. A fruitgrower may want to get a new kind of fruit. He may cross two kinds he has in the hope of getting one. The tangelo is a cross between a tangerine and a grapefruit. The plumcot is a cross between an apricot and a plum.

Fruits are of no use to a plant unless they have seeds in them. But for eating, seedless fruits are pleasant, and some seedless fruits have been developed. There are now seedless grapes and seedless oranges. Bananas have no seeds—only tiny black dots left from what were once seeds. There are seedless watermelons, too. In time there may be many other seedless fruits.

Should a tomato be called a fruit? This is a question people often argue about. A scientist would say yes. For scientists call any package in which a plant puts its seeds a fruit. To them, a pod of peas, a squash, and a cucumber are fruits, too. But a tomato does not have enough sugar in it to be called a fruit by most people. Neither does a pea pod or a squash or a cucumber. (See APPLES; BANANA; CITRUS FRUITS; DATE; FOODS; GRAFTING; GRAPES; HYBRIDS; PLANT BREEDING; PLANT FACTORIES; VEGETABLES.)

Cherries
Cranberries
Blueberries
Apple
Persimmon
Plums
Mango
Navel Oranges
Figs
Red Raspberries
Peaches
Lemons
Strawberries
Watermelon
Bananas
Grapes

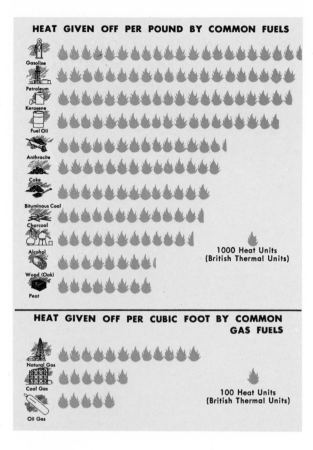

HEAT GIVEN OFF PER POUND BY COMMON FUELS

Gasoline

Petroleum

Kerosene

Fuel Oil

Anthracite

Coke

Bituminous Coal

Charcoal

Alcohol

Wood (Oak)

Peat

1000 Heat Units
(British Thermal Units)

HEAT GIVEN OFF PER CUBIC FOOT BY COMMON GAS FUELS

Natural Gas

Coal Gas

Oil Gas

100 Heat Units
(British Thermal Units)

FUELS For heating our buildings, cooking our food, and running our machines we depend chiefly on the burning of fuel. Even when we use electricity for heating and cooking and running machines, we can in many, many cases trace the electricity back to a power plant in which fuels are burned to drive the electric generators.

Butter and sugar and walnuts will burn. But nobody buys them as fuels for his stove, furnace, or automobile. They are too expensive. A fuel for common use must be fairly cheap. Besides, it should give off a great deal of heat when it burns.

The chart names 14 common fuels and shows how these fuels compare in the amount of heat they produce. It shows, for instance, that a pound of hard coal, or anthracite, gives off about twice as much heat as a pound of peat.

A fuel may be a solid, a liquid, or a gas. Gas and liquid fuels have one advantage over solid fuels: they leave no ashes.

But, like solid fuels, they may give off gases that pollute the air.

Some fuels are natural fuels. Coal, wood, and natural gas are among them. Other fuels are man-made. Gasoline and kerosene, for instance, are made from petroleum, coke and coal gas from coal. Coal, natural gas, and the fuels from petroleum are often called fossil fuels. They came in the beginning from living things of ages ago.

The giant rockets that launch satellites need special fuels—fuels we would not think of using for everyday purposes. Liquid hydrogen is one rocket fuel. It gives off a tremendous amount of heat as it burns.

Scattered over the world there are now many nuclear power plants. In them reactors produce heat used to drive steam turbines which in turn drive electric generators. The "fuel" used in these reactors is not like most fuels—it does not burn. The heat it gives off comes instead from the splitting of its atoms. One nuclear fuel is uranium 235. A pound of this fuel produces over two and a half million times as much heat as a pound of coal! (See COAL; NATURAL GAS; PETROLEUM.)

FULTON, ROBERT (1765–1815) It was the 17th of August, 1807. A crowd stood along the banks of the Hudson in New York City waiting for a boat to start up the river. The boat was the one we know now as the "Clermont." It had a steam engine instead of sails to make it go. Robert Fulton had planned it and had it built. Almost no one expected the big new riverboat to work. As it got under way Fulton heard such mocking shouts as, "Bring us back a chip of the North Pole." To the crowd's surprise the boat went chugging up the river on its way to Albany. Hats began to sail into the air and there were many cheers. Thirty-two hours later the boat tied up at Albany. It was a success.

Fulton was born in Pennsylvania. As a boy he was interested in drawing. By the time he was 21, he was making a living by

STEAM FERRY

STEAM BATTLESHIP

R. FULTON

TORPEDO

SUBMARINE NAUTILUS

painting portraits. Then he decided to go to England to study with the famous painter Benjamin West.

Through West, Fulton met many interesting people. Some of his London friends were interested in navigation. Fulton became interested, too. He was interested chiefly in canals at first, then in submarines. Later he became interested in steamboats. He built one and tried it out near Paris. It was a failure. He built another and tried it out. This one worked.

An American friend urged him to plan a steamboat for use on the Hudson, and Fulton did. The boat was the "Clermont."

Fulton's steamboats were not the first ones ever made. John Fitch was one of several men who had built earlier steamboats that worked. But because the "Clermont" was the first one to be really successful, Fulton is generally called the inventor of the steamboat. (See BOATS; ENGINES, HEAT; INVENTIONS; SUBMARINES.)

FUNGI (FUN jy) Most people think of the color green when they think of plants. But there are thousands of kinds of plants that are not green. Most of these thousands of plants are fungus plants, or fungi.

Fungi are simple plants. They do not have roots, stems, leaves, or flowers. They never bear seeds. Most of them are small compared with a bush, a tree, or even a cabbage plant. Some are much too small to be seen without a microscope.

Unlike plants that are green, fungi cannot make their own food. Instead, they must get food from animals or from other plants. Some get their food from living plants or animals. The others get their food from dead plants or animals or from such plant and animal products as flour, sugar, lumber, and leather. Some fungi, by their ways of getting food, cause a great deal of trouble.

Mushrooms are the largest of the fungi. You see only the spore-bearing parts of

Inky Cap   Meadow   Sulphur

THREE COMMON MUSHROOMS

the three mushrooms in the picture above. Spores serve mushrooms as seeds. The main part of a mushroom plant is a mass of colorless threads called a mycelium. The mycelium of the inky cap, like that of the meadow mushroom, is in the ground. The mycelium of the sulphur mushroom is hidden in the trunk of the tree. Some mushrooms, as you probably know, are good to eat. But some are very poisonous.

The bread and jelly molds are much like mushrooms except that they are smaller. They have a fuzzy colorless mycelium and tiny stalks that bear spores. There are other molds, too. All molds are fungi.

The mildews that grow on lilac and rosebushes are fungi. So are the rusts that sometimes ruin whole fields of grain. Yeasts are fungi, too. They are far too small to be seen with the naked eye. Lichens, amazing plant pioneers that can grow on bare rock where no other plants can get a foothold, are made partly of fungus threads.

Some fungi, like the rusts and mildews and poisonous mushrooms, we can consider our enemies. But others are helpful. And some, although we do not use them directly, play an important part in the world of living things. Some, for instance, help make dead plants and animals decay. (See DISEASE GERMS; LICHENS; MOLDS; MUSHROOMS; PARASITES; PLANT KINGDOM; YEASTS.)

FUNNY BONE At the back of the elbow there is a place where a nerve comes close to the surface: there is not much padding to protect it. This place is call the funny bone. When a person strikes his elbow against something, he may hit his funny bone. Then his whole arm tingles. The tingling is not at all pleasant. The name "funny bone" gives the wrong idea.

FURNITURE Long ago, when people had to wander about to hunt for food, they did not have any furniture. Perhaps they sometimes dragged in a stump to serve as a stool or a log for a bench. But they could not carry furniture about with them. Even today there are tribes of nomads, or wanderers, who have almost no furniture because they have only tents as homes.

It was different after people tamed animals and learned to raise crops. Then they could live year in and year out in one place and could have better homes. They began to build furniture for their homes.

At first people thought only of the usefulness of furniture. But in time the idea grew of making it beautiful as well as useful. By the time the Egyptians were building their great pyramids they were also making beautiful furniture. Some of it was decorated with gold and inlaid with ivory. There were soft cushions for chairs. Of course, not all Egyptians had furniture of this kind. Only nobles did. We know about it because such things as chairs, couches, and chests for clothes were buried with the nobles in their tombs. In museums today some of this furniture can be seen.

Pictures tell the story of furniture better than words. The pictures here show furniture of different times and places.

Differences in national customs explain some of the differences in furniture. No one today lies down to eat, as many of the ancient Greeks and Romans did. We do not, therefore, have dining couches as they had. Since we do not use roll books, no one now needs a cabinet for them.

Inventions have brought new pieces of furniture into our homes. Floor lamps and television consoles would be completely strange to the people of early times.

Some of the early furniture was carved out of stone. But stone furniture is heavy and hard to move. We find it now chiefly in gardens, where it can stay in the same place all the time. Wood has been the chief material for furniture down through the centuries. Some kinds of wood have been especially wanted because of their beautiful color and their hardness. Oak, mahogany, ash, beech, walnut, teak, cherry, and maple have all been much used. Now metals and plastics are also being used for furniture. Many chairs and sofas have thick cushions of foam rubber. In some cases the whole framework of the chair or sofa is covered with thick padding and then with cloth, leather, or plastic.

Ideas about beauty are not the same in all parts of the world. And in the same part of the world styles in furniture change just as styles in clothes do. At many times and in many places the best furniture has been much carved and decorated. At other times plain furniture has been best liked.

Designing beautiful furniture is an art. Many furniture makers have become famous. Among them are Thomas Chippendale, George Hepplewhite, and Thomas Sheraton, 18th-century furniture makers of England.

Duncan Phyfe was a furniture maker of the United States who became famous for his work in the early 1800's.

There are still furniture makers who have their own small shops and do much of their work by hand. But most of today's furniture is made in large factories. Making and selling furniture is now a very big business. It amounts to hundreds of millions of dollars a year. The city in the United States that is best known for the mass production of inexpensive furniture is Grand Rapids, Mich. Grand Rapids is sometimes called the furniture capital of the United States.

STYLES OF FURNITURE

Modern Bench and Cupboard

Early American Cupboard

Sheraton Table

Four-poster Bed

Louis XV Chair

Modern Chair

Renaissance Chair

Pennsylvania Dutch Chest

Modern Coffee Table

Colonial Secretary

Early American Butterfly Table

Ancient Egyptian Stool

Duncan Phyfe Sofa

Roman Stone Chair

Ermine

FURS Long ago people in cold countries began wearing furs to keep warm. Later, kings and queens decorated their robes with fur to show that they were rulers. Now furs are common. Millions of people wear them for both warmth and beauty.

A great many animals have coats of fur. But the fur of some is much more beautiful than that of others. The fur of some, more-over, wears especially well.

The fur of the sable is the aristocrat among furs. The best sable comes from Siberia. At one time only the members of the royal family of Russia were allowed to wear it. Some animals change their coats with the season. The ermine does. In the summer it is brown so that it matches the ground. In the winter it is white so that it matches the snow except for a black tip on its tail. White ermine fur came to be a favorite for royal robes. Chinchilla is one of the rarest and most delicate of all furs. It comes from a dainty little animal of South America. The beaver, mink, musk-rat, fox, and seal also furnish us with excellent fur. Rabbit fur is not as durable as most furs, but it is much used.

Fur trapping and trading have had a great deal to do with opening up new lands. Fur traders were the leaders in exploring much of North America. Many of its present-day cities were early fur-trading posts. New York, St. Louis, and Quebec are three of them.

Today much of the fur that is bought and sold comes from fur farms. About three-fourths of all the mink, for instance, is so-called ranch mink. Chinchillas and foxes are other mammals raised for their fur. (See BEAVER; CHINCHILLA.)

Platinum Mink

Blue Mink

Alaska fur seals are big—they sometimes weigh 600 pounds. Every fall they leave their breeding grounds in the Pribilof Islands in the Bering Sea and swim south. They return in spring.

Mink live near water and feed on fish and other water animals.

The letter G has the same history as the letter C, for C and G both began as the same letter. It probably came in the beginning from the picture of a camel. The letter was the third one in the Greek alphabet. The Greeks called it *gamma*. They wrote it in these ways: Γ ᑯ C . The Romans wrote it in its rounded form. They first used the letter for both the sound of *g* and the sound of hard *c*, or *k*. Finally they made a new letter by adding a short stroke to indicate the *g* sound.

Our letter G stands for three sounds. It has a different sound in each of these words: *engine*, *gone*, and *mirage*. G is silent in some words. *Gnome* is one of them.

GALAGO (ga LAY go) The little animal in the picture is a galago. Galagos are rather close relatives of the aye-aye and the tiny tarsiers. They are found wild only in Africa and on some nearby islands. There are several kinds. The largest are about the size of cats. The smallest are smaller than squirrels. A common name for galagos is "bush babies."

Galagos are pretty with their woolly fur, bushy tails, big ears, and big eyes. They are among the animals that can turn their heads enough to look straight behind them.

As one would guess from its big eyes, a galago usually hunts for its food at night. It eats mostly fruit and insects. During the daytime it curls itself up in a tree. A man who once had a pet bush baby said that it used to wrap itself in a newspaper every morning and sleep until dusk.

Bush babies make good pets. But they are not as intelligent as their big eyes make them appear. Their way of finding out about anything new is to chew it. A person who has a pet galago may expect to have his ears and fingers chewed a bit.

These little animals can move fast. On the ground they hop like kangaroos. In the trees they leap remarkable distances from one branch to another.

At night it is not hard to tell when there are galagos nearby. Their cries as they hunt for food are a common night sound of the African bush. (See AYE-AYE; MAMMALS; TARSIER.)

Great Nebula in Andromeda

GALAXY A galaxy is a vast star city or island universe. It is made of millions and millions of stars. The galaxy in the picture is the shape of a hamburger bun with flattened edges. This galaxy is one that we see when we look in the direction of the

Spiral Galaxy Seen Edgewise

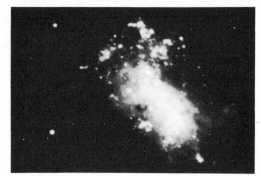

Irregular Galaxy

constellation Andromeda. Another name for this kind of galaxy is spiral nebula.

Photographs of this nebula in Andromeda are taken through a powerful telescope. Without a telescope this great star city can hardly be seen. Although it is made up of millions of stars, it is so far away that without a telescope the whole galaxy looks like one faint, fuzzy star.

Our sun with all its planets is a part of a galaxy called the Milky Way Galaxy. In the Milky Way there are about 100 billion stars. Scientists are sure that it is about the shape of the Great Nebula in Andromeda. But of course no one can go out beyond it to take a picture of it.

No one knows exactly how many hundreds of millions of galaxies there are. Each bigger telescope made has brought more galaxies into view. The great Hale telescope on Mount Palomar added many to the list. Some of them are so far away that it takes light from them five billion years to reach us. As you see, not all galaxies are the same shape. (See MILKY WAY; UNIVERSE.)

GALILEO (1564–1642) The man who came to be called the father of science, Galileo Galilei, lived in Italy over 300 years ago. At the time he lived, most people got their ideas about science from books written centuries before. Galileo wanted to find things out for himself. He began carrying on experiments.

When Galileo was only 17, so the story is told, he was standing one day in the cathedral of Pisa, the city in which he lived. Above his head a lamp hanging by a chain was swinging back and forth. As it swung, it sometimes moved only a little way, sometimes much farther. Galileo noticed that, no matter how far it moved, the swings always took the same time. He timed them by counting his pulse. Watching this lamp led Galileo to study the pendulum, for a lamp on a chain is really an example of a pendulum. His work paved the way for making the first good clocks.

While he was teaching mathematics at the University of Pisa, Galileo proved that the old idea that heavy objects fall faster than light ones is wrong. Legend says that he dropped two balls of different weights from the top of the Leaning Tower of Pisa. To the surprise of most people, the balls hit the ground at the same time.

As soon as Galileo heard of a new invention called a telescope, he set about making telescopes for himself. With them he made many discoveries. He was the first person to see mountains on the moon and sunspots on the sun. He discovered that the planet Jupiter has moons traveling around it. He discovered that the planet Venus seems to change shape. He found that the band of light called the Milky Way is the light from a vast number of distant stars. All that he saw made him sure that the great scientist Copernicus was right in saying that the earth is not the center of the universe—that it is one of the sun's family of planets and moves around the sun. He wrote a number of books about his ideas.

Galileo made himself unpopular because he dared to doubt the learned people of earlier times. For his last eight years he was even imprisoned in his own home for some of his beliefs. But he accomplished a great deal. He started scientists to finding out for themselves new things about the world around us. (See COPERNICUS.)

GALLS Nearly everyone has seen a gall. Hardly an oak tree stands that does not have several "oak apples" hanging from it. These are the work of gall wasps. Midges and plant lice are other insect gallmakers. Bud mites, tiny relatives of spiders, cause galls also. Galls are made by fungi, bacteria, and viruses, too. Altogether there are more than 2,000 kinds of galls.

Usually the kind of gallmaker can be told from the looks of the gall. Each makes a particular form of gall. Some galls are smooth, some rough. Some galls are single. Others are in clusters. Many gallmakers

(Cutaway View)

Oak Gall

Goldenrod Galls

Blackberry Knot Gall

make galls on only one family of plants. They may be even more particular. Some choose only one special part of the plant. Of the wasps that cause galls on oak trees, 275 choose leaves, 175 stems, 45 buds, 41 roots, and 55 acorns.

A gallmaker causes galls by irritating plant tissues. An oak apple is made in this way: The gall wasp lays eggs on an oak leaf. A wormlike larva hatches from each egg and begins to eat. As it feeds, it is thought to give off from its mouth a juice which irritates the leaf. The leaf begins to grow faster where it is irritated and soon grows completely around the larva. The larva is now surrounded by a lacy network of living plant tissue that serves as both food and shelter.

In most cases the gallmaker does no real harm to the plant. Several kinds of galls are useful. Many oak and sumac galls are used for inks and dyes. Oak apples are fed to livestock. Most useful of all galls are the nodules on the roots of some legumes. The bacteria in them help change nitrogen from the air to a form green plants can use. (See DYES; INK.)

Ring-necked Pheasant

Mallard Duck

Wild Turkey

GAME BIRDS People raise many birds for food. Many wild birds, too, are good food. They are called game birds. Hunting these birds is a popular sport.

Many game birds spend most of their time on the ground. Among them are quail, grouse, turkeys, and pheasants. Other game birds are water birds. Among them are wild ducks and geese.

In the early days of America game birds were plentiful. They were killed a few at a time all year round by both white settlers and Indians. Later, hunters began killing more than they needed for themselves and selling them. Game birds began to grow scarce. Some, like the passenger pigeon, disappeared entirely.

Then in some places people began to raise such game birds as quail and turn them loose. Laws were passed, too, to protect game birds. The period when a certain kind of bird can be killed is called open season for that bird. Even in the open season there is a limit to the number of birds a hunter may bag. And some game birds cannot now be hunted at all. If hunters obey the laws, there should continue to be good hunting without killing off any kind of bird. (See QUAIL; WATER BIRDS.)

Most game birds are hunted in the fall after they have laid their eggs and raised their young. Many sporting dogs are trained to help in hunting.

Ruffed Grouse

GAME FISHES No fish is called a game fish unless it puts up a good fight after it has taken a fisherman's hook. Most fishes are caught for food. But game fishes are often caught just because men enjoy the fun of catching them.

Big game fishing is done in salt water. Here such huge fishes as the tuna, marlin, and swordfish are found. They may weigh hundreds of pounds! Two other large salt-water game fishes are the tarpon and the sailfish. These fishes are famous for their jumping. The tuna, marlin, tarpon, and sailfish are very fast swimmers.

Sharks sometimes spoil big game fishing. They ruin the catch by taking bites out of a fish before it can be reeled in.

Channel bass, weakfish, and bluefish are among the smaller saltwater game fishes. They are all good fighters.

The muskellunge is the king of freshwater game fishes. A muskie may weigh over 60 pounds. Muskies are found in lakes and rivers in northern United States. Other freshwater game fishes are the smallmouth bass, walleye, pickerel, and northern pike.

Brook Trout

Rainbow Trout

Trout are the favorite fishes of the fly-fishermen. Fly-fishermen use artificial flies as bait for the fish they want to catch. Trout live in cool lakes and streams. A trout fisherman thinks nothing of getting up early in the morning and standing in cold water for hours to catch one of these speckled beauties. (See FISHING.)

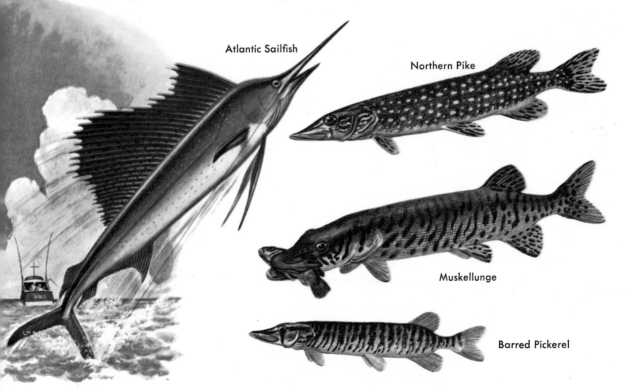

Atlantic Sailfish

Northern Pike

Muskellunge

Barred Pickerel

Sculling

Polo

Baseball

Football

Archery

Lacrosse

Skating

Skiing

Boxing

Mexican Ring Ball

Pole Vaulting

Jai Alai

Golf

Tennis

Jumping Rope

Leapfrog

Walking on Stilts

Rolling Ho

Piggy-back Joust

Seesaw

Marbles

Blindman's Buff

Spinning Top

GAMES AND SPORTS All over the world children play games—card games, ball games, singing games, and others besides. Many grown people play games, too. In some games each person is for himself. In others there are teams. Some games are quiet. Others are very lively.

Every game has its own rules. And every one is a kind of contest. Winning and losing are always a part of playing a game.

No complete list could be made of all the games people play, for new ones are being thought up all the time. But some of our games are as old as history.

Games that take a great deal of athletic skill are often called sports. Baseball, jai alai, and tennis, for instance, are sports. Some games are especially popular in some parts of the world, others in other parts. There are also sports such as hunting and mountain climbing that are not games.

Most sports call for special equipment. There are many sporting goods stores.

Checkers

Dominoes

Backgammon

Sports that are fun to watch as well as to play are often called spectator sports. A hundred thousand people may watch a single football game or a boxing match.

Games and sports are more than fun. Team games help the players learn to get along with one another. All games help the players learn to be good winners and good losers. And many games and sports help in building strong bodies.

The ancient Greeks believed so much in athletic contests that they started the Olympic games. Americans believe in athletics so much that almost every school now has a planned program of sports and games. (See ATHLETICS; MARBLES; OLYMPIC GAMES; WINTER SPORTS.)

GARDEN FLOWERS The five flowers in the pictures on this page and the next are common in our gardens. They were common in our grandmothers' gardens, too. There are many other garden flowers.

Some garden flowers are tall plants. Some are short. Many of the plants stand straight all by themselves. But some are vines and have to have fences or poles to climb on. As everyone knows, the flowers themselves are not all the same shape or the same size or the same color. There are other ways in which they are different. Many, for instance, have a perfume all their own. People like roses and lilacs and lilies of the valley as much for their perfume as for their beauty.

Some garden flowers live much longer than others. Some grow from seed, bloom, and produce seed all in one year. These plants are called annuals. Some flowers grow from seed one summer, die down for the winter, and then grow up again and bloom the next summer. These flowers are called biennials. Some flowers are hardy. They live for more than two seasons. These flowers are called perennials. Since there are many different climates, flowers that are hardy in one place may not always be hardy in another.

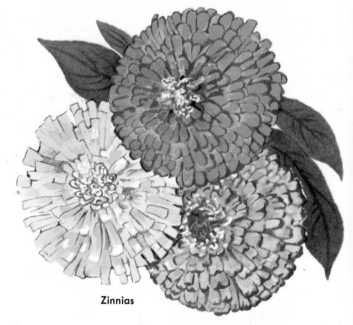

Zinnias

Four of the five flowers in the pictures are annuals—zinnias, nasturtiums, petunias, and cornflowers. They have to be planted every year. Often some annuals that need a long growing season are planted early in the spring indoors. They get a head start in this way. When the weather is warm enough, the little plants can be transplanted out of doors. Pansies and petunias are often started indoors.

Most hollyhocks are biennials. They bloom the year after they are planted.

Many hardy flowers are raised from bulbs or roots or cuttings rather than from seed. Tulips are among the perennials that we commonly raise from bulbs.

Some garden flowers are very particular about the kind of soil they grow in. Sweet peas, for instance, will not grow well unless they have very rich soil. Zinnias, on the other hand, will grow in poor soil. But zinnias are particular about sunshine. They do not grow well in shade. It pays, then, to ask a few questions about every flower you are considering for your garden:

How long does it live?

Does it need a fence or a pole to climb on as it grows?

In what kind of soil does it grow best?

Is it sun-loving or shade-loving?

The United States has often been called a melting pot because people have come to it from all over the world. American flower gardens are melting pots, too. If gardens in America had only flowers that are natives of America, they would still be beautiful with their roses and azaleas and California poppies. But they would not be nearly as beautiful as they are now. In American gardens of today petunias and morning glories and nasturtiums from South America grow side by side with zinnias and marigolds from Mexico and snapdragons from Europe. Glads from Africa can be found growing beside chrysanthemums and hollyhocks from Asia and strawflowers from Australia.

Every year seed companies send out catalogs telling what kinds of flowers they have to sell. Why must there be new catalogs every year? We would not need new flower catalogs every spring if flowers were not being improved year by year. Roses were common in grandmother's garden, but we can buy kinds of roses that our grandmothers never heard of. Flower growers are always working to get better varieties of our common garden flowers. Most of our flowers are now very different from their ancestors that once grew wild. (See FLOWER; FLOWER FAMILIES; GREEN-HOUSE; HYBRIDS; ROSES; SEEDS; WILD FLOWERS.)

GARDENS, FAMOUS Twenty-five centuries ago in Babylon there were beautiful gardens growing on high terraces. These famous Hanging Gardens were one of the Seven Wonders of the Ancient World. All down through the centuries and in many lands there have been famous gardens.

There are many different types of gardens. And, although to most people a garden means flowers, a garden to be beautiful does not have to have flowers. The old Italian garden pictured gets much of its beauty from the spacing and shaping of trees and shrubs. A Japanese garden has few, if any, flowers. Instead, it has stones, streams, bridges, and evergreens.

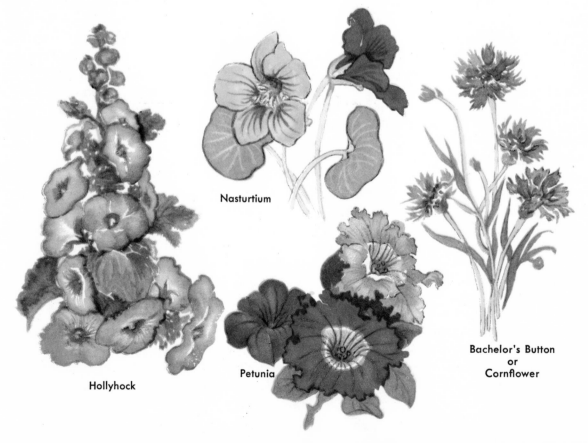

Nasturtium

Hollyhock

Petunia

Bachelor's Button
or
Cornflower

Italian Garden

Japanese Garden

Magnolia Gardens

Cypress Gardens

The gardens of Versailles, near Paris, are often called the most beautiful gardens in the world. They have magnificent fountains and terraces as well as beautiful trees and flowers. These gardens surround the great palace of Versailles, where some of the kings of France once lived.

Kew Gardens are on the edge of London. In these gardens there are plants from all over the world. Queen Victoria gave Kew Gardens to the people of England.

The Cypress and Magnolia Gardens near Charleston, S.C., are two of many famous American gardens. The trees of Cypress Gardens are bald cypress trees. Long moss hangs down from them. The water in the lake that winds through the garden is black because of minerals in it. It acts as a mirror. This garden is most beautiful in the early spring when the trees are just leafing out and the thousands of daffodils along the paths are in bloom. Magnolia Gardens are almost as famous for the azaleas and camellias blooming there as for the magnificent show of magnolias each spring.

Bellingrath Gardens near Mobile, Ala., are in bloom the year around. Camellias, azaleas, dogwood, and gardenias are a few of the great variety of flowers there. Many of the trees in this one-time plantation are live oaks, which are evergreen. They, too, are festooned with long moss.

Not all famous gardens are large. Rockefeller Center Garden is small as gardens go. The plants in it are raised somewhere else and then brought there. Beginning with crocuses in early spring, they end at Christmastime with a giant Christmas tree. This garden in the heart of huge New York City is perhaps seen by more people in the course of a year than any other. (See ROCKEFELLER CENTER.)

GEMS For thousands of years people have worn gems, or jewels. Gems were bought and sold in ancient Babylon at least 4,000 years ago. The ancient Egyptians sent expeditions to nearby lands for gemstones. Strings of beads have been found even in the graves of prehistoric people.

Gems are costly because they are rare. Of the many kinds of gems, a few are so rare and valuable that they are called precious stones—chiefly the diamond, ruby, sapphire, and emerald. Other gems are called semiprecious.

Diamonds are the best liked of all gems. They are prized chiefly because of their brilliance. Diamonds are crystals of carbon. The finest come from Africa.

Turquoise · Diamond · Ruby (Gem) · (Crystal) · Topaz · Opal · Amethyst · Aquamarine · Zircon · Garnets · Emerald · (Crystal) · (Gem) · Sapphire (Gem)

Rubies, sapphires, emeralds, topazes, zircons, amethysts, aquamarines, and garnets are crystals, too. They are crystals of several different minerals. Crystals of gem minerals are not used as they are found. Jewelers cut them to make them more brilliant and beautiful.

Rubies and sapphires are crystals of the same mineral. It is called corundum. The beautiful colors of these gems come from impurities in the corundum.

Big rubies are among the rarest and most beautiful of gems. They are rarer than big diamonds. For centuries the finest rubies have come from Burma. Sapphires are found in Burma, too, and also in many other places. Star rubies and sapphires are especially prized. When cut properly they show inside them a six-pointed star.

Rubies and sapphires more nearly perfect than those found in nature can now be manufactured. They are not considered precious stones since they are not rare. Diamonds can also be manufactured, but they are not of good enough quality to be called gems.

The emerald is a lovely rich green color. In ancient times there were famous emerald mines near the Red Sea. Today the finest emeralds come from the mines of Colombia, in South America.

Emeralds are crystals of the mineral beryl. So are aquamarines. Aquamarines are not as beautiful, rare, or expensive as emeralds. Like most of the gems in the picture, they are semiprecious stones.

Amethysts are crystals of the common mineral quartz. Quartz comes in many different colors. It is not called amethyst unless it is lavender or purple.

The topaz pictured is yellow. But topazes are not always yellow. They may be blue, green, brown, or even deep red. The best topazes come from Brazil.

The name "garnet" comes from the old Latin word for pomegranate. Garnets were supposed to look like pomegranate seeds. Most of them are deep red, but there are brown, yellow, green, black, and orange garnets, too. Much old-fashioned jewelry is set with garnets. Garnets are not as popular as they used to be. Some of the best garnets come from the United States, although garnets were worn in the Old World long before America was discovered.

Some zircons look much like diamonds. They are colorless crystals. But the most prized are red or yellow. Most zircons come from Ceylon and Indochina.

Opals are quartz, but they are not crystals. They do not flash their color because of any coloring matter in them. Instead, their color comes from the way tiny cracks in them break up the light that strikes them. Many people think that the opal, because of its flashes of color, or fire, is the most beautiful of all gemstones. Mexico and the United States produce fine opals. The very finest come from Australia.

Of all gem minerals none has been used more widely or for a longer time than turquoise. Turquoise is found in a great many parts of the world. The finest comes from Iran. There have been turquoise mines in that region for as long as there have been any records. The ancient Egyptians mined turquoise, too. Much beautiful turquoise is mined in the southwestern part of the United States. The Indians of the Southwest use a great deal of turquoise in making jewelry and ornaments.

Pearls are quite different from other gems. They are not mined. Instead, they are formed inside the shells of pearl oysters and their relatives.

There are a great many superstitions about gems. Diamonds were once supposed to protect their wearers from danger. Rubies were supposed to bring love and happiness. Emeralds were believed to bring wealth and fame and to be a help in foretelling the future. Amethysts were supposed to give wisdom. Most of us no longer believe in such superstitions. Today most precious stones are worn simply because they are beautiful. (See BIRTHSTONES; DIAMONDS; PEARLS; QUARTZ.)

GENGHIS KHAN (JENG gis KON) (1162–1227) Many people call Genghis Khan the world's greatest conqueror. He conquered more of the world than did either Napoleon or Alexander the Great.

"Genghis Khan" is not a name. It is a title instead. "Genghis Khan" means "greatest of rulers." "Khan" means "ruler." The real name of this ruler was Temujin. He was a Mongol. His home was in the vast desert region of Asia called Mongolia.

It took Temujin many years to earn his title of Genghis Khan. But he was a ruler when he was just a boy. His father, the chieftain of a tribe of Mongols, died when Temujin was 13, and the boy, therefore, became the new chieftain.

The tribe began at once to dwindle. His people did not want a young boy for a leader. Many of them left to join other tribes. Once a neighboring tribe captured him, but he escaped. Little by little he rebuilt his tribe. At last he and his men were able to conquer the tribes round about. By the time he was 44 he was the ruler of all Mongolia. Then he got his title of Genghis Khan.

But he was still not satisfied. He wanted to conquer more of the world. He took his thousands of Mongol soldiers to fight against China. For a time the Great Wall of China stopped him. But he finally conquered most of the country, which in those days was called Cathay.

Genghis Khan then led his Mongols into India, Afghanistan, and Persia and on toward the Mediterranean Sea. Still he was not satisfied. He led them on into Russia. But in the midst of his victories Genghis Khan died. He left to his heirs a vast empire and the fiercest of armies. The famous Kublai Khan was his grandson. (See MARCO POLO.)

GENIUS A genius is a person who, because of his great ability and accomplishments, towers far above his fellowmen. He may be an artist or scientist or inventor. He may write music or poetry. He may have other gifts. Geniuses are often so deeply interested in one thing that they do not pay much attention to anything else. Many of them are thought of as strange.

Albert Einstein was surely a genius. Much of what he thought and wrote has to do with great problems about the universe. His ideas helped to bring on the Atomic Age. Thomas Edison earned the name of genius by his many inventions. Newton, Galileo, Mozart, Shakespeare, Michelangelo, and Leonardo da Vinci are a few of the other geniuses the world has known.

GEOGRAPHY All the hundreds of millions of people in our world live on less than one-third of the surface of the ball-shaped earth. Water covers more than two-thirds of that huge curved surface.

The regions where people live differ in many ways. A homeland may be level or mountainous, wet or dry, hot or cold. The soil may be fertile or poor. The region may be crowded with people or there may be very few. It is clear that in different homelands people do not face the same problems. The people of Tibet, high up in the Himalayas, cannot live just as the Indians live along the Amazon. The way of living the Eskimos have worked out in the Arctic would not fit the Sahara.

People change the lands where they live by adding such things as buildings and roads, bridges and dams. They cut down forests, plant fields, and mine for minerals.

In geography we learn about differences in the lives of people in different homelands and about things which help us understand those differences. About any homeland we ask questions such as: What ways of making a living have people found here? What changes have people brought about? How do the skills and ideas they have gained in trying to meet their needs and solve their problems differ from those of people in other lands? How do people in other lands depend on them and help them?

Maps are very important in geography because they tell many facts which are needed in answering such questions. In their special sign language maps show how such things as highlands and lowlands, rainfall, farmlands, forests, minerals, and people are distributed. (See MAPS.)

GEOLOGY What is the earth made of? How did it come to be as it is? The science that answers these questions is geology. Rocks, minerals, fossils, earthquakes, volcanoes, caverns—these are some of the things geologists study. They study, too, the battle between land and sea that has been going on since the earth was young. They find out how mountains are formed and how they may be worn down.

The earth is made up of rocks of many kinds. In some places the rocks are arranged in layers. These rock layers are like pages in a great book. Geologists learn to read them just as most people read pages of printing. The rocks tell geologists about changes in climate, ancient lava flows, and changes in land and sea. Fossils embedded in the layers of rock make these rocks into a kind of picture book.

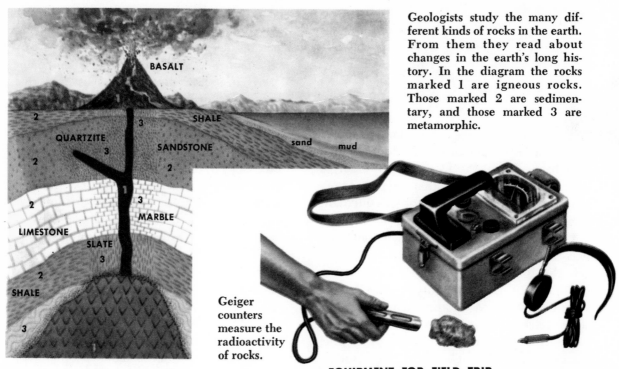

Geologists study the many different kinds of rocks in the earth. From them they read about changes in the earth's long history. In the diagram the rocks marked 1 are igneous rocks. Those marked 2 are sedimentary, and those marked 3 are metamorphic.

Geiger counters measure the radioactivity of rocks.

EQUIPMENT FOR FIELD TRIP

Geology is so big a science that it is divided into many smaller sciences. Each of these smaller sciences has its own name. If a person is especially interested in the living things of long ago, he studies paleontology. If he is interested in minerals, he studies mineralogy. If he wants to know more about earthquakes, he studies seismology. There are still other branches.

Among the questions the geologists of today are interested in are these: Were all the continents once joined together? Are they slowly drifting now? Is the Ice Age over or are we merely in a stage between two advances of the ice? What secrets about earth history do the unexplored floors of the oceans hold?

People do not usually study geology just for the fun of finding out more about the earth. What geologists know can be put to many practical uses. Finding new deposits of oil, planning ways to keep rivers from stealing our soil, and choosing good places for tunnels and dams are among them. The work of geologists often takes them to faraway places. (See EARTH HISTORY; FOSSILS; MINERALS; ROCKS.)

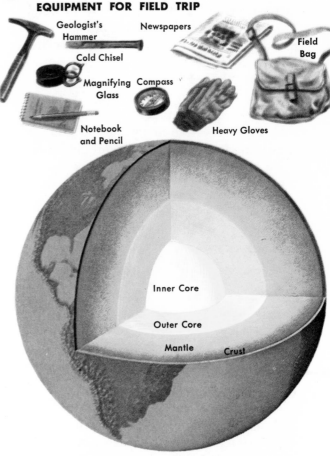

CUTAWAY VIEW OF EARTH

GEORGIA The region making up the southeastern corner of the United States is sometimes called the Deep South. Georgia is one of the states of that region. Many songs and stories tell of Georgia's pleasant climate, and of its beauty, too.

Georgia was one of the 13 colonies. It was the last of these colonies to be settled, but the fourth to enter the Union. It became a state in 1788. Georgia is the largest state east of the Mississippi River. Fourteen states have more people.

Georgia was named in honor of George II, an English king. The first English settlement in Georgia was made by General James Oglethorpe in 1733. He brought with him a band of poor folk. They chose a place on the coast for their home. The settlement was named Savannah. Savannah was founded just a year after George Washington was born in the oldest colony, Virginia.

Soon settlers from many European countries came to Georgia. They were drawn by word of the religious freedom there and of the rich red soil. Wealthy planters from other southern colonies also came, bringing their slaves with them. They laid out big plantations on the Piedmont, a plateau in north-central Georgia. Farther south, on the sandy coastal plain, farmers raised cattle and hogs in forest clearings.

Many thousands of the people of Georgia still earn their living by farming. Cotton is their best money crop. Farmers have learned to use the sandy soils of the southern half of the state for peanuts, pecans, tobacco, watermelons, peaches, and early vegetables. Georgia produces more peanuts and pecans than any other state. In watermelons it ranks third. Its peach crop is so big that "Peach State" is one of Georgia's

nicknames. Georgia leads all the states in the production of broilers.

Another nickname for Georgia is "Empire State of the South." It gets this name partly from the importance of its factories. Factories now bring more wealth to Georgia than farming. Most of Georgia's factories are in or near Piedmont cities. The factories get all the power they need by using Piedmont rivers and the coalfields of the southern Appalachian Mountains. For raw materials they use products from the farms and forests, and from the state's great granite and marble quarries. The chief factory and mill products are cotton cloth, cottonseed oil, peanut oil, peanut butter, and lumber. The biggest industrial cities are Atlanta, Savannah, Columbus, Augusta, and Macon. Atlanta, the state capital, is Georgia's most important railroad center. With its more than 500,000 people, it is Georgia's largest city.

In 1861, at the beginning of the Civil War, Georgia withdrew from the Union. It was readmitted in 1870.

Among the many highlights in Georgia's history are these: In 1793 Eli Whitney, while visiting a cotton plantation near Savannah, invented the cotton "gin"—short for "engine"—a machine to separate rapidly the cotton seeds from the fibers. His cotton gin helped to boost cotton production all over the South. In 1819 the first steamship to cross any ocean sailed from Savannah to England. In 1927 Franklin D. Roosevelt established the famous foundation for the treatment of polio in Warm Springs.

Georgia's state tree is the live oak. Its motto is "Wisdom, justice, and moderation," and its state song, "Georgia."

Golf at Augusta

Paratrooper, Ft. Benning

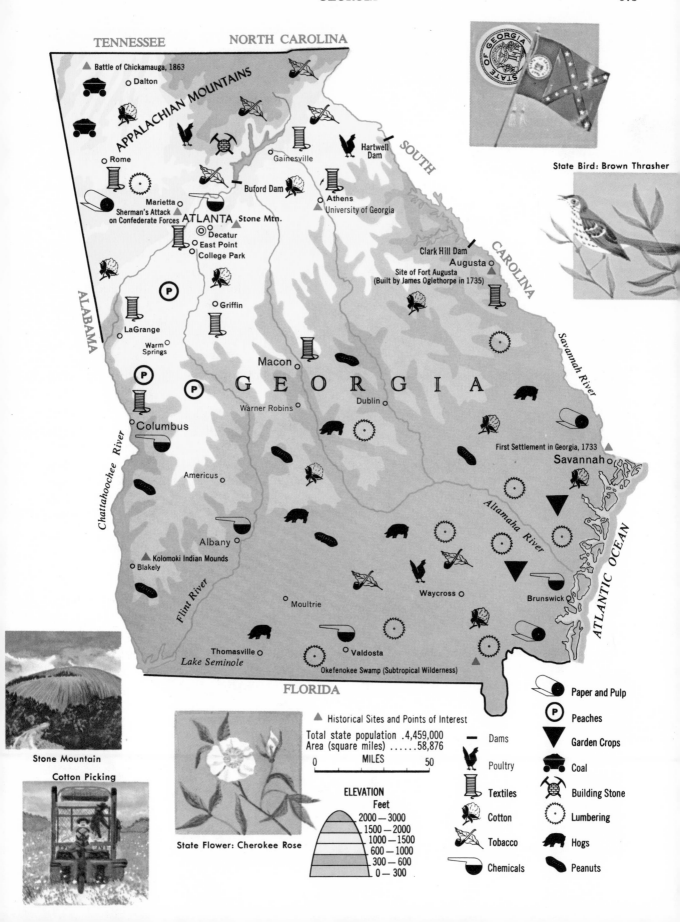

TENNESSEE

NORTH CAROLINA

SOUTH CAROLINA

ALABAMA

FLORIDA

ATLANTIC OCEAN

State Bird: Brown Thrasher

▲ Battle of Chickamauga, 1863
○ Dalton

APPALACHIAN MOUNTAINS

○ Rome

Hartwell Dam

Gainesville ○

Buford Dam

Marietta ○
Sherman's Attack on Confederate Forces

ATLANTA
Stone Mtn.

○ Decatur
○ East Point
○ College Park

Athens ○
University of Georgia

Clark Hill Dam
Augusta
Site of Fort Augusta
(Built by James Oglethorpe in 1735)

○ Griffin

LaGrange ○

Warm Springs ○

Macon

GEORGIA

Savannah River

Columbus ○

Warner Robins ○

Dublin ○

First Settlement in Georgia, 1733

Savannah

Americus ○

Altamaha River

Albany ○

Chattahoochee River

▲ Kolomoki Indian Mounds
○ Blakely

Flint River

Waycross ○

Brunswick ○

Moultrie ○

Thomasville ○
Lake Seminole

Valdosta ○
Okefenokee Swamp (Subtropical Wilderness)

Stone Mountain

Cotton Picking

State Flower: Cherokee Rose

▲ Historical Sites and Points of Interest

Total state population .4,459,000
Area (square miles) 58,876

MILES
0 ————————— 50

ELEVATION
Feet
2000 — 3000
1500 — 2000
1000 — 1500
600 — 1000
300 — 600
0 — 300

— Dams

🐓 Poultry

🧵 Textiles

🌿 Cotton

Tobacco

Chemicals

Paper and Pulp

Ⓟ Peaches

▼ Garden Crops

Coal

Building Stone

Lumbering

🐖 Hogs

Peanuts

GERMANY Before 1871 there were many rather small German states. In that year they united to form the German Empire. Among the states was Prussia. The king of Prussia became the emperor, or kaiser, of the big new Germany. Berlin, in Prussia, was made the empire's capital.

Although much of the land in Germany was swampy and the growing season was short, many Germans were farmers. Some were fishermen. Others worked in the forests. Still others worked in the cities, which were centers of trade.

Before long the new country was on its way to becoming a great industrial nation. It was rich in coal and iron ore and had other materials mills and factories needed. In its universities important scientific discoveries were being made. Soon there were great steel mills in Essen and cities nearby. Chemical plants and factories of other kinds sprang up in many cities.

Rivers and canals were improved. Railroads and broad highways were built, many of them centering on Berlin. At the same time that industry was growing, swamps were being drained and steps were being taken to improve the farmland. Before World War I Germany had become a great trade, farming, and manufacturing country.

Germany and its allies were defeated in World War I. After the war the country became a republic. But before many years Adolf Hitler, leader of the Nazis, rose to power. Under his dictatorship, Germany started a war that became World War II. Again Germany and its allies lost.

At the beginning of World War II Germany was Europe's fifth largest country.

Since the war it has been a divided land. The northeastern part is called the German Democratic Republic, or East Germany. It is closely tied to the Soviet Union and the other Communist countries of eastern Europe. No governments except those of the Communist countries recognize it as an independent nation. The rest of Germany is the Federal Republic of Germany, or West Germany.

West Germany is about two-thirds as large as prewar Germany. Its capital is Bonn, a city on the Rhine.

Nine European countries are larger than West Germany. But none except the Soviet Union has more people. The country is very crowded. There are 12 cities of more than 500,000, and three—West Berlin, Hamburg, and Munich—have over a million.

Nearly 3,000,000 of West Germany's workers are farmers or foresters. Several times as many are miners, builders, or factory workers. The country's chief exports are manufactured products, among them chemicals, yarns, automobiles, bicycles, and cameras. The leading crops are potatoes, sugar beets, wheat, rye, barley, oats, and grapes for wine. Cattle, pigs, and poultry are the main kinds of livestock. Fishermen add to the country's food supply by catching half a million tons of fish each year. But food is an important import.

Germany has much to interest tourists. There are medieval castles and cathedrals, famous universities, the busy Rhine with terraced vineyards along its banks, and great trade fairs and music festivals. (See BERLIN; EUROPE; HISTORY; NAZIS; WORLD WAR I; WORLD WAR II.)

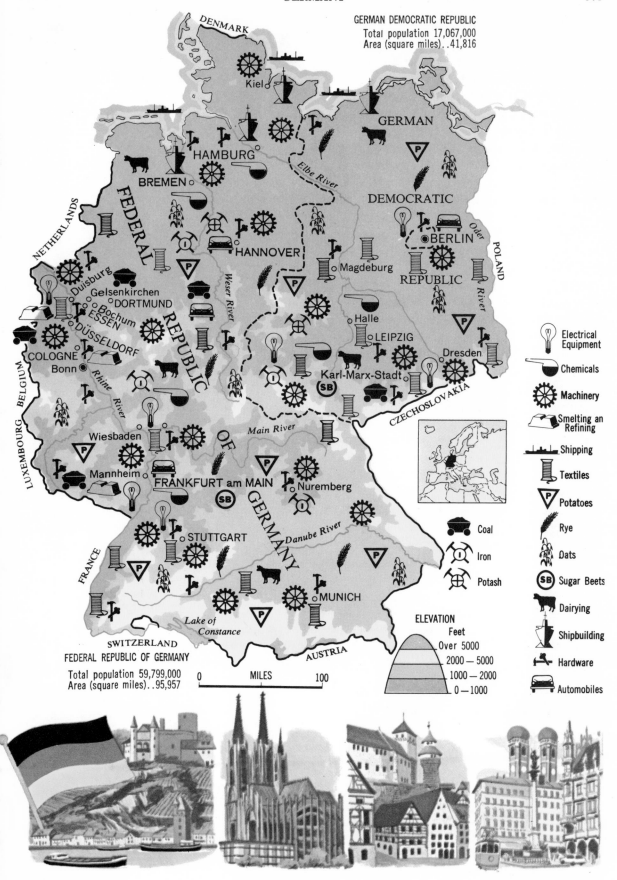

GERMAN DEMOCRATIC REPUBLIC
Total population 17,067,000
Area (square miles)..41,816

DENMARK

Kiel

HAMBURG

GERMAN

BREMEN

FEDERAL

Elbe River

DEMOCRATIC

HANNOVER

BERLIN

Oder River

POLAND

Magdeburg

REPUBLIC

Duisburg

Gelsenkirchen
DORTMUND
Bochum
ESSEN
DÜSSELDORF

Weser River

Halle

LEIPZIG

Dresden

COLOGNE
Bonn

Rhine River

Karl-Marx-Stadt

CZECHOSLOVAKIA

NETHERLANDS

BELGIUM

LUXEMBOURG

Main River

Wiesbaden

OF

Mannheim

FRANKFURT am MAIN

Nuremberg

GERMANY

FRANCE

STUTTGART

Danube River

MUNICH

SWITZERLAND

Lake of
Constance

AUSTRIA

FEDERAL REPUBLIC OF GERMANY
Total population 59,799,000
Area (square miles)..95,957

0   MILES   100

Legend:

- Electrical Equipment
- Chemicals
- Machinery
- Smelting and Refining
- Shipping
- Textiles
- Potatoes
- Rye
- Oats
- SB Sugar Beets
- Dairying
- Shipbuilding
- Hardware
- Automobiles
- Coal
- I Iron
- Potash

ELEVATION
Feet
Over 5000
2000 – 5000
1000 – 2000
0 – 1000

GEYSER A geyser is a special kind of hot spring. Hot water does not flow from a geyser all the time as it does from ordinary hot springs. Instead, a geyser is quiet for a time. Then it suddenly erupts and shoots water high into the air.

For a geyser, there must be hot rock not far below the surface of the ground. There must also be a narrow, crooked passage leading up from the hot rock.

The eruption of a geyser comes about in this way: Water fills the crooked passage. The water at the bottom gets very hot. If the passage were big and straight, the cold water at the top would gradually sink down and push up the hot water. As it is, the hot water is bottled up. It gets so hot that it begins to boil and form steam. The steam pushes some of the cold water out of the top of the tube. As soon as a little comes out, there is less cold water to press down on the hot water. The hot water then changes to steam very fast and shoots the water above it up into the air.

Geysers are found in only a few places. There are about 200 in Yellowstone National Park in Wyoming. Most of the others are in Iceland and New Zealand.

The most famous geyser is Old Faithful in Yellowstone Park. It erupts every 65 minutes or so. Visitors seldom have to wait more than an hour to see Old Faithful perform. (See HOT SPRINGS.)

Old Faithful